"Every once in a while, a book shifts our perspective of what life, love and leadership are all about — it's ALL about creating value! Based on the groundbreaking science of applied neuro-axiology, this book reveals the how-to principles for integrating your heart, mind, and brain to unleash your strengths and create a truly extraordinary life."

> ~ Stephen R. Covey,
> author, *The 7 Habits of Highly Effective People*
> and *The Leader in Me*

"*Answering The Central Question* is spot on and right to the point. For anyone who wants to maximize value in their personal life, their organization, or the quality of life on this planet, this is the book to read, study and apply. It says it all! Once a person employs these tools, so generously shared with the reader, their improvement will be obvious and noteworthy. Readers who study, apply and live these principles, will find greater joy in life and increase their self-respect. They will feel glad to be alive, living with purpose, and proud to be part of the answer, not the problem."

> ~ Marvin Katz, Ph.D.
> Author, *Ethics as Science*
> Former Director, World Future Society – Midwest Region

"Peter and Harvey break down the immensely complicated subject of personal values into smart language to help anyone become a better, more accomplished person! *Answering The Central Question* provides the bedrock backbone for clarity in setting a new roadmap for personal and professional success."

> ~ Tom Schulte, Exec. Dir., Linked 2 Leadership
> CEO, Recalibrate Professional Development

"This book is truly groundbreaking! It reveals the connection between mind and brain, science and spirit in a compelling, practical way. In the field of personal, leadership and organizational development this book reveals a rare and wonderful new paradigm for unleashing human potential, especially your own."

~ Lisa Kramer, MSW, PCC
Author, *Loving With Intention*: A Guide for Relationship Coaching
Faculty Member, Executive Coaching Program, University of Texas
President, Living with Intention, LLC

"This book has the power to actually change the way you operate in the world. I have read at least 300 books in the self-help, success genre. What's amazing about this book is that it combines real science in simple to understand language with powerful insights and tools to help you to create sustainable success in your life. What's more, it elicits a deep level of inspired self-motivation within the reader, which will move you into action. I highly recommend this read."

~ Ken D. Foster, CEO - Premier Coaching,
Bestselling Author, *Ask and You Will Succeed*

"These pages contain the wisdom of the ages and the opportunity of a lifetime. Through 'The Central Question,' Peter and Harvey hand us a compass to navigate beyond the pain and suffering of the human condition; opening our hearts to embrace humanity. As a chiropractor I see the science, art, and philosophy of the book being put to use every day with unlimited benefits showing up like miracles in my life and my practice."

~ Sandy Johnson, Chiropractor

"This book is about the truth that is in every man and woman. 'The Central Question' brings true freedom; one no longer has need to chase after every wind of self-discovery and success."

~ David Njau

"*Answering The Central Question* breathes new life into the age-old quandary of how to tap into our limitless human potential. The authors' fresh thinking, sound ideas, and scientific basis can add immense value to everything we do. This book offers a special set of keys to unlock the potential in all of us."

~ Jeff Levy
Director, Center for Strategic Leadership
Dale Carnegie Training of Long Island

"This book explains the cutting-edge science of applied neuro-axiology in practical terms and provides readers with powerful tools that change lives. Centering questions are so simple, yet so amazingly powerful in helping people to think through their decision making process and be assured that they make good choices – every time. *Axiogenics* has great promise for increasing human potential. It's an exciting new world!"

~ Julie Donley (Fuimano)
Personal Leadership Coach
Author, *The Journey Called YOU,
A Roadmap to Self-Discovery and Acceptance*

"In *The Fifth Discipline*, Peter Senge's message was: 'we are prisoners of our own thinking.' *Answering The Central Question* teaches us how to liberate ourselves from the thinking that holds us back! This work has been instrumental in my becoming top ranking among my peers."

~ Hugh J. Campbell, CPA

Answering
The Central Question

How Science Reveals the Keys to Success
in Life, Love and Leadership

Authored by:

Peter D. Demarest
and Harvey J. Schoof

PHILADELPHIA

Answering The Central Question

How Science Reveals the Keys to Success in Life, Love and Leadership

Published by:

HeartLEAD Publishing LLC,
www.Heartleadpublishing.com
info@heartleadpublishing.com

Contact publisher for additional books, to buy in bulk, corporate edition inquiries, bookstore distribution, or to request author information for speaker, media or other requests.

Visit www.Axiogenics.com for information regarding commercial applications and professional services based on the content of this book.

Susan Kaminga, Editor
Charlon Bobo, Editor, EditCopyProof
Cover design by Peter D. Demarest

ISBN: 978-0-9827102-1-0
Library of Congress Control Number (LCCN): 2010917673
Printed in the United States of America
1 3 5 7 9 8 6 4 2 0

Dedications

To my parents, Marcia and Don Demarest, I dedicate this book in gratitude for their unwavering faith, unconditional love, the exquisite example they set, and the invaluable life-lessons they gave me, which admittedly, may have taken me far longer to learn than they may have preferred.

Mom, I hope heaven has a good bookstore with a cozy place to curl up and read, and that reading this book makes you proud of what you've accomplished.

-Peter

I dedicate this book to my loving and patient wife Jan, who has always given me the room to pursue my dreams, and to my three children: Kris, Pat and Sue, who have taught me how to become a valuegenic human being.

-Harvey

Disclaimer

Peter and Harvey are not therapists or psychologists. The contents are solely the opinion of the authors and should not be considered as a form of therapy, diagnosis or treatment of any kind: medical, spiritual, mental or other. Any choices or actions taken by the readers, or result from reading or discussing and acting upon anything contained in this book, are completely the responsibility of the reader. The authors, publishers, contributors, and distributors make no promises, warranties or guaranties as to the fitness and suitability of this book's content for any specific use, purpose or application whatsoever.

The authors look forward to the day when making such a systemic disclaimer as this is unnecessary. Moreover, they contend that these disclaimers are prudent because some people do not understand the very principles contained in this very book.

As compensation to the reader for holding the authors and related parties harmless, regarding what the reader or anyone else does with the content of this book, the authors and related parties lay no claim or entitlement to any of the benefits that the reader may experience, or the success and abundance they may create as a result of reading this book and applying the principles and practices it contains, so long as all intellectual property rights are honored in accordance with appropriate law.

All of the stories and examples in this book are based on real people and real situations However, most names have been changed to protect privacy and some of the elements of the stories have been changed for editorial purposes.

Table of Contents

Preface

"Now I know why nobody likes me," Beth said, "even though they all pretend they do." It was the first day of a two-day workshop and the group just returned from an afternoon break. Beth was a senior project manager who came to the workshop to find out how to get people to do what she needed them to do. That morning we explored basic principles of axiology (value-science). We completed an exercise that illustrated how—even with the best of intentions—we can unknowingly crush other people emotionally. She discovered that it was *she* who was not being who *they* needed her to be and it was sabotaging her effectiveness.

Tim, a self-made millionaire, was in tears. After an hour of going over his "VQ" assessment report, he suddenly understood why his wife, Patti, had left him a few months earlier. For 24 years of marriage, he had treated their marriage more as if she was an employee or minority business partner than a wife and equal partner. In Patti's world, she could never live up to his expectations no matter what she did. Every day was a failed attempt to please him. Long ago, she had sacrificed her own dreams. Patti resented Tim for that.

True, financially, Tim provided more than she could ever have imagined, but she was empty inside; an emptiness that no amount of money, or the things money could buy, would ever fill. Now that the children were grown and out on their own, her duty fulfilled, she had no good reason to stay. Money was certainly not an issue. The boys didn't really like coming home for visits anyway.

Tim also realized that there were many people in his life that he treated much the same way he had treated Patti. Of course, most of them were his employees. Many of them had left him as well.

After several months of coaching, Tim was a changed man. He had set himself free of most of his old mental programs and learned to tap into his real strengths. For the first time in his life, he understood the real value and meaning of love, compassion, and partnership.

It took time, patience, and tremendous effort, but he was able to establish a new relationship and a "new" marriage with Patti. The kids returned home often to bask in the love of the old newly-weds. What's more, Tim became even more effective as business leader, yet more relaxed, self-confident, and peaceful inside.

"I never would have believed it," John admitted. "This one issue damn-near destroyed our company. In two hours you accomplished what we hadn't been able to accomplish in three years and tens of thousands of dollars paid to other consultants." John was the CEO of a company created out of a merger of two competing companies with very different approaches to the same business. The culture had become so toxic that there were actually fistfights in the hallways. Nothing seemed to work. They tried personality testing, executive retreats, bonding experiences, behavior modification programs, emotional intelligence (EQ) trainings and workshops, and the list goes on. Each time, things would be good for a few days, but eventually the old problems would emerge again.

John shared these comments of feigned disbelief with me several months after I worked had with his executive team. There were no more fistfights, cooperation and teamwork were at an all-time high, and the working environment had gone from toxic to engaging. The few people who had resisted the change had left the company and there were no signs of the old problems coming back. The company truly had transformed. Rhetorically he asked me, "Why don't more people understand this stuff? [Meaning what I had taught his team.] Why didn't I know about this a long time ago?" Well John, it's time to let the world know.

The preceding are just three examples of why we've written this book. Everyday people needlessly suffer, companies waste precious resources, and society deals with the fallout, all because most people don't understand the real principles of value generation. Moreover, most of the methods and techniques for "self-improvement" that the "success guru's" have been selling simply don't work for most people because they don't align with how the mind-brain actually works. This book intends to change all that.

Everyone has what it takes to create greater success and abundance in their lives. For most people, just a few habitual thought processes, perspectives, and perceptions stand in the way of liberating their greater potential. Everything we need to create greater success is already right between our ears; all we need are the keys to unlock it.

Beth, Tim, and John are just three examples of what happens in lives and organizations when people embrace and apply the principles this book articulates. Our greatest hope for this book is that it opens a similar door for you and your organization.

We invite you to read this entire book with a curious and open mind. Use your intuition and reasoning to test these principles against your own life experiences.

This work is not about promoting any moral, ethical, or religious agenda other than to help you generate greater value. Regardless of your spiritual beliefs, profession, cultural foundations, social status, or education, what you will learn in this book applies to every aspect of your life.

Our intention is to articulate the philosophy, science, principles, and practices that help people become masters at "*Answering The Central Question.*" No matter how large or small your aspirations, this book could bring about a critical turning point in your life. Using these principles, you can change your life, transform your organization, and bring immeasurably greater value to the world.

We are honored that you have undertaken reading this book. In truth, it speaks far more about you than it does about us. It speaks to your commitment to being the best you can be. May it bring tremendous value to you and everyone you touch.

~ *Peter D. Demarest and Harvey J. Schoof*

CHAPTER 1

Introduction

"Try not to become a man of success
but rather try to become a man of value."

~ Albert Einstein

"The greatest waste in the world is the difference between
what we are and what we could become."

~Ben Herbster

The Central Question

This question is at the heart of every human endeavor.

"You don't want a million answers as much as you want a few forever questions. The questions are diamonds you hold in the light. Study a lifetime and you see different colors from the same jewel."

~ Richard Bach

Life is about adding value. Whether you realize it yet or not, your entire life is about one thing: creating value. Virtually every thought, action, choice, and reaction you have is an attempt to create or preserve value.

Success in life, love and leadership requires making good value judgments. Real personal power is in knowing which choices and actions will create the greatest net value. The greater the quality of your choices and actions, the greater success you can have personally and professionally.

To that end, this book is all about learning how to answer what we call The Central Question of life, love, and leadership:

**"What choice can I make and action can I take,
in this moment, to create the greatest net value?"**

The better you can learn to answer this question the more value you can create and the more success and happiness you can achieve.

Answering The Central Question is not about forcing yourself to do things you don't want to do. It's about getting very clear about what you *really* value, making good choices, and then taking appropriate actions. It is not about fixing your "weaknesses," it's about *liberating* your strengths. It's not about sacrificing yourself; it's about recognizing and celebrating your own value equal to all others. It's not about *getting* greater value; it's about *creating* greater value.

This kind of thinking is what we call a "valuegenic" mindset: a deliberate intention to generate greater net value. Unfortunately, most people approach life from a perspective that is more about getting what they want than about the value they can generate. If you really want to get more of what you want, the key is to think about how you can *create* greater value rather than about the value you can get.

While asking yourself The Central Question is an essential first step, it is just the beginning. If you want to maximize your success and happiness, then you'll need to learn more about the science, principles and practices of being valuegenic. If you are a leader who wants to maximize the success of your organization, or a parent who wants to give your children the keys to a successful life, or a partner who wants to create an extraordinary, loving relationship, keep reading.

• • •

Introduction to Axiogenics™

Two previously disconnected sciences integrated into a cutting-edge new technology for personal, leadership, and organizational development.

Axiogenics™ is, "the mind-brain science of value generation." It is a practical life-science based on *applied neuro-axiology*[1] — the integration of neuroscience (brain science) and axiology (value science).

Neuroscience is the study of the biochemical mechanics of how the *brain* works. We are, of course, primarily interested in the human brain, which, owing to our genetics, is one of the most complex and magnificent creations in the known universe.

Axiology is the study of how Value, values and value judgments affect the subjective choices and motivations of the *mind*—both conscious and sub-conscious. *Formal* axiology is the mathematical study of value—the nature and measurement of value and people's perception of value.

Both axiology and neuroscience have existed separately for years. In many ways, the two sciences have approached the same question (What

---

[1] A term first introduced to the world in a short whitepaper called: *Neuro-Axiology: A Foundation for Value-Centered Leadership and Organizational Development* (Demarest, Schoof, Blanchard, © 2008, 6 Advisors, Inc.)

makes people tick?) from opposite directions. Neuroscience, a relatively young science, seeks to understand *brain* function and explain human behavior from a neuro-biological perspective. In contrast, for 2500 years, axiologists have sought to understand and explain human behavior and motivation from the perspective of the moral, ethical, and value-based judgments of the *mind*.

Many human sciences, including neuroscience and axiology, have come to the realization that the mind-brain is value-driven. That is, Value, values, and value judgments drive many, if not most or even all, of the processes of both the brain and the mind, including our sub-conscious habits of mind. Think about it—have you ever made a conscious choice that wasn't, at that moment, an attempt to add greater value at some level?

Unfortunately, to our knowledge, the neuroscientists and axiologists have not been comparing notes. Consequently, until now, the amazing *value-based* connection between the mind and brain has been overlooked. This book makes that connection and more.

Axiogenics is not some rehashed mystical, moral, or religious philosophy, nor is it a newfangled twist on the rhetoric of so-called "success gurus." It is a fresh, new paradigm for personal, leadership and organizational development. It is a science-driven technology for deliberately creating positive changes in how we think, how we perceive, the kinds of choices we make, and the actions we take.

Axiogenics is based on four core principles. They are:

1. Value drives success in all endeavors.
2. Your mind-brain is already value-driven.
3. There is an objective, universal Hierarchy of Value.
4. Accurately answering The Central Question is the key to maximizing your success.

You've already learned about The Central Question, and if you simply started asking it of yourself several times a day, you would most likely begin noticing results rather quickly. The Central Question is a powerful first step that will help you engrave a valuegenic perspective on your heart and mind.

However, there is much more to Axiogenics and The Central Question than you may realize. Training your mind-brain to *answer* The Central Question consistently and accurately is another level of mastery entirely. Your mind can be both your greatest asset and your greatest liability. By understanding these core principles and then applying the science-based practices prescribed, you'll be able to unleash more of the potential of your existing strengths to maximize value. Simultaneously, you will be minimizing the negative impact of old mental programs and habits that may be sabotaging your efforts. Using this process, you can master both the heart *and* science of generating value.

· · ·

Success

> Success in one area of your life does not have to come at the expense of success in another.

How do you define success? Clearly, success comes in many forms: wealth, relationships, social, competitive endeavors, spiritual clarity, parenting, leadership, sales . . . the list can go on and on.

According to the dictionary, to succeed means "*to accomplish what is attempted or intended.*"[2] Is there any part of your life where asking The Central Question would be inappropriate? Is there any place in your world where creating greater value would not be a good thing and a worthy goal?

Axiogenics is about creating greater success in *any and all* of life's endeavors. You can use these principles and practices to improve any area of your life that you choose: personal or professional. However, our deepest hope is that you will come to understand that real success can

---

[2] succeed. Dictionary.com. *Dictionary.com Unabridged.* Random House, Inc. http://dictionary.reference.com/browse/succeed (3/20/2010).

only be achieved when net value is maximized everywhere in life. The Central Question is not about making more money, being the best parent, or inspiring others to greatness. It's about creating the greatest possible net value: everywhere, all the time. It encompasses your career, finances, relationships, community, and family roles as well as your spiritual, physical, and emotional wellness.

We must recognize that true success can only be maximized when others are successful as well. For example, a true leader succeeds by leading in a way that enriches the lives of their followers.

Everyone has the potential to reach higher levels of success. You maximize success by optimizing the value you create in your life *and in the lives of others*. This book is about unleashing your *valuegenic* potential: the potential we all have to generate greater net value. Axiogenics is the methodology: the science-driven, strengths-focused principles and practices that make it all possible.

• • •

Perspective and Perception

> Our unique power to value things from multiple perspectives—in multiple dimensions—is what enables us to reason, to make value judgments and choices, and even to change our minds.

"When you change the way you look at things,
the things you look at change."

~ Wayne Dyer

Imagine yourself on the ground looking up into a tree. What do you see? What do you feel? How would you describe the experience?

When looking up at the tree you might be pleased by the subtle shifts of the leaves caused by a light breeze. You might feel a sense of awe at the majesty of the tree and be aware of its perfect structure as you look up at the whole of it.

Now imagine yourself as high up as you can climb in that tree look-ing down. Now, what do you see? Now, how do you feel? Now, how would you describe the experience?

When up in that tree, your perception of the light breeze turns into something quite different as the branch on which you stand sways back and forth. You might feel fear, trepidation, or outright terror as you look down, down, down to the ground far below. Your emotional state might be so keyed up that you can't really think about or see anything else but the ground and the branch to which you cling. Even from atop the tree, if you are clinging to old-ways of thinking, your vision and, therefore, your possibilities, may be limited.

Yet, what if you allowed yourself to raise your sights and look beyond your doubts, fears, or concerns? You might be surprised to discover a whole new world of possibilities and a path that could lead you beyond the horizon of your self-imposed limitations.

That path to a world of possibilities has always existed. To see it, all that needs to change is your perspective. When your *perspective* changes, your *perception* changes as well. This is the fundamental dynamic of all deliberation, reasoning, discernment, judgment, valuing, deciding, etc.—seeing from different perspectives.

For example, have you ever had an argument with yourself? Think about it—what is the nature of an "argument," but that there are two (or more) different perspectives on the same issue? Consider the seemingly never-ending battles in the United States Congress. Politicians on both sides of an issue may agree that something needs to be done, but each side has a different perspective on the subject—they see things diffe-rently; they value things differently. This same dynamic goes on be-tween your ears, thousands of times per day.

Decisions are based on value perspectives and perceptions. How often has your perception of something shifted when you've made the effort to look at it from a different perspective? How often has this change in perspective resulted in a change in the value you placed on something?

Your value perspectives are created from your life experiences and engrained in the neuropathology of your habits. Most people recognize that they have a few "bad" habits or tendencies. Things like negative self-talk, procrastination, reactive responses, sloppiness, disorganization, laziness, or feelings of obligation plague many of us. Conversely, most people also have many positive attributes and have developed at least a few good habits and ways of seeing things (perspectives) that support their success and happiness.

As you can see, perspective and perception play a major role in life. It makes sense that the more accurate your perception, the more effective you can be in your choices and decisions.

• • •

VQ

> VQ or "Value-judgment intelligence Quotient," is the capacity to make good value judgments—to be valuegenic.

Part of what differentiates Axiogenics from other approaches to personal development is the ability to quickly and objectively identify and measure a person's current capacity to think valuegenically.

All of your choices, plans, and actions are based upon how you judge the value and potential value of everything in your life, including what makes you *you*. Your VQ (Value-judgment intelligence Quotient) is the driving force behind those judgments.

The science of axiology provides a practical means for objectively measuring your VQ from 36-unique value perspectives. Those perspectives that score the highest are your strengths—thought processes that best enable you to answer The Central Question accurately. Knowing at least some of your VQ profile also allows you to:

- apply customized practices to optimize your thinking,
- eliminate "weaknesses" and their negative influence,
- unleash your potential to generate greater value, and

- take advantage of your brain's natural ability to create new, positive habits in permanent support of your greater success.

As such, the measurement of VQ is a key element in applying the technology of Axiogenics. Later in the book, we will explain exactly what VQ is, how it is measured, and why understanding your VQ profile is so important. For now, just know that *VQ is your capacity to accurately perceive and judge value from any of 36 different perspectives.*

. . .

Unleashing Potential

You can unleash 40% more productivity!

"If your actions inspire others to dream more, learn more, do more and become more, you are a leader."

~ John Quincy Adams

In words immortalized by the U.S. United Negro College Fund (UNCF) in 1971, "A Mind is a Terrible Thing to Waste." The human mind has capabilities far beyond what most people allow themselves to believe or that most work environments typically allow people to explore or express. The result is a huge loss of potential and a waste of talent, productivity, and creativity.

Dr. Robert Hartman, the "Father" of formal axiology, demonstrated over four decades ago that when the principles you will learn are instilled in an organization's culture, cooperation and productivity increase by an *average* of 40%.[3]

If you are a leader, you have the opportunity to unleash this potential by creating a valuegenic organization. No matter how successful your organization may already be, what would be possible if you could unleash 10%, 20%, or 40% more of your people's potential? Would it

---

[3] (R. S. Hartman 1963)

impact profitability? Would it improve morale, loyalty, and the ability to attract even more talent?

In Chapter 7, *The Valuegenic Organization*, we'll examine axiogenic principles in the context of organizational culture and change. We will look at the benefits, both tangible and intangible, for becoming an organization with a valuegenic mission and culture.

Regardless of your professional role, job, title, or position, you are a leader; you have influence. If you are a parent, you are a leader. If you are a friend, you are a leader. Leadership is not just about position, title, and authority; it's about empowering and influencing others such that they willingly unleash more of their own greatness.

The Central Question is a leadership question. It demands an answer that unleashes potential value through choice and action. It fosters accountability and responsibility. Even in the face of failure, the question calls us forth to learn, grow, and keep going. Are these not the attributes of a leader?

We invite you to read this book from the perspective of *first* using these principles as the "leader of one"—your Self. Use these principles to unleash the fullness of your own potential. This will prepare you to model and apply these principles to your organization, family, relationships, and community as the leader of many.

> "Most people live, whether physically, intellectually or morally, in a very restricted circle of their potential being. They make very small use of their possible consciousness, and of their soul's resources in general, much like a man who, out of his whole bodily organism, should get into a habit of using and moving only his little finger."
>
> ~ William James

• • •

What Kind of World Do You Want?

Our world is on the cusp of a transformation. We have the opportunity and the technology to unleash the fullness of the human spirit. But, do we have the will? Do YOU have the will?

"We must become the change we want to see."

~ Mahatma Gandhi

Axiogenics is a *technological* advance, not a philosophical one. It is the integration of newly discovered scientific knowledge. Technological advances allow us to create new products, systems, and methodologies that are intended, ultimately, to improve quality of life. Some advances are relevant only to a few people in specific niche environments, professions, or life circumstances. Axiogenics, however, is applicable to virtually all people because it deals with the very essence of what it means to be human.

Axiogenics provides a universal framework for maximizing value in all things. By adopting a valuegenic approach to all personal, business, social, economic, ethical, and political decisions, humankind can uphold and unleash all the goodness that progress can create while mitigating the risks of collateral damage. At the same time, Axiogenics sheds new light on the age-old quest for higher meaning, purpose, values, ethics, and morals.

Our world, your world, is on the cusp of another transformational time—a renaissance of sorts. At one end of the spectrum, great and divergent political forces are driving wedges between science and spirit. At the other end, science and spirit are finding more commonality and convergence with each other than ever before.

The Western Renaissance of the 14th to 16th centuries was a time of great change and gave birth to the modern era. It was the time of such lauded thinkers as Newton, Galileo, da Vinci, Copernicus, Mirandola, Shakespeare, Machiavelli, and Descartes. Yet it was also the time of the Inquisition, the Hundred Years War, slavery, and the black plague. It was a time of great change as old empires collapsed new ones were born.

Today, technology and communications are demolishing the barriers that geography, culture, religion, politics, and even industrial-might have long imposed. The global landscape is dramatically and rapidly changing.

More and more we see organizations comprised of people from every race, language, custom, religion, and world-view working shoulder to shoulder. On any given day, millions of people travel to faraway lands to interact with people of very different cultures than their own. What's more, this "travel" need not be any farther than our computers and cell phones.

The co-mingling of diverse value perspectives is creating new social, business, and political dynamics. For some, this brings excitement and possibility: for others, uncertainty, fear, and even destruction. Organizations that were the stalwarts of finance and industry just a few years ago, no longer exist. Old "empires" are crumbling and new ones are emerging. The question is, will the new empires be any better than the old ones?

At the same time, technological and scientific advances are bringing us ever-closer to understanding the enormously important continuity and interdependence between all things, from the infinite immensity of the cosmos to the infinitesimal smallness of quantum physics.

People have become keenly interested in exploring and discovering the greater meaning and purpose of life. The ideals of social responsibility, stewardship, and servant leadership are taking center-stage in the world theater of commerce and politics.

Yet in the face of all this transformation, our global economy is troubled, our ethics are being tested, and our sense of meaning and purpose is being strangled by conflict and the need for financial survival. Many people are stressed and fearful of an unknown future. Too many of our leaders and policy makers are showing themselves to be extraordinarily self-centric and arrogant while masquerading as having our best interest at heart.

Which direction will the world go? Where will we be ten, twenty, fifty years from now? There are powerful forces at work that doubt the fundamental goodness of the human spirit. These forces do not trust human nature. Some seek to control and limit our freedoms. Clearly, history has given ample evidence that human nature can have a "dark side." We know that human nature is greatly influenced by life experiences, cultural norms, education, conditioning and even indoctrination. However, science has also shown that biologically "normal" human brain prefers and seeks goodness.[4]

What if humankind could shift from the prevailing self-centric mindset to a mindset that holds The Central Question in the forefront? Could we alter the current trajectory of our global future?

Could we embrace our local and global diversity while coming together toward common goals as individuals, groups, teams, organizations, nations, and world-citizens? Could the "hard" world of science converge with the "soft" world of love, respect, spirituality, Values, morals, and ethics, rather than remain segregated by fear, hatred, and a struggle for power? What will it take to create thriving and abundant businesses, communities and societies in the face of those that would seek to limit and control human nature?

The first Renaissance marked the beginning of the segregation between science and spirit and gave rise to an age of polar opposites, such as religious fervor and scientific elitism, liaise faire capitalism and authoritative communism, imperialistic domination and self-protective isolationism. The science and principles in this book can provide the foundation for a new and very different kind of renaissance. Axiogenics holds the promise of a re-convergence; a middle ground based in hard science, yet anchored in the innate Values and goodness of the human spirit.

We *can* maximize net value by unleashing human potential, rather than suppressing it and coercing people into making the decisions that

---

[4] (Pugh, 1977)

those in power want them to make. We *can* shift our thinking to be more focused on creating value: celebrating and unleashing all the good that our creative human *spirit* brings to life and still be logical and rational. Unlike the *Star Trek* character, Mr. Spock, we *can* choose to be both rational-logical and loving-compassionate.

Can we afford *not* to shift ourselves and our culture towards a more valuegenic way of life? If we fail to make this shift, we may find ourselves no better off than we were in the dark ages. Under the control and influence of self-centric power brokers and policy makers, apathy and mediocrity will only get worse and ultimately lead to the destruction of individuality, personal choice, creativity, and self-determination.

The human spirit is hungry for goodness. The human mind is amazingly adaptable and pre-wired for incalculable goodness. The world is starving for more enlightened leadership. We know we can be better and we *must* be better if we are to fulfill our true potential.

What kind of world do you want? You have the power to choose. If you are the only one in the world that continually seeks to answer The Central Question, it may only make a difference within your immediate circle. But you are not alone and you have more influence than you may know.

The world you choose to work towards is your children's world. You have the power to choose what kind of legacy you want leave them. If enough become intentionally more valuegenic, we *will* change the course of history. You will reap your own rewards of freedom and abundance, and together we will create a strong foundation for future generations to build upon.

You can start by learning to understand and embrace the principles of living, loving, and leading from the perspective of The Central Question. Making this shift will require doing the work to develop your own capacity to answer the Question: to unlock and raise your own VQ.

Community and organizational leaders can model and apply these principles to unleash the enormous reserves of human ingenuity, productivity, partnership, and cooperation locked within the prison of self-centric doubts, fears, and concerns. A global renaissance will require a multitude of like-minded people dedicating themselves to the task and encouraging others to do the same. It will require personal discipline and a collective commitment. In the face of resistance from those that would seek to limit and control the full expression of our human spirit's innate potential for greatness, we will need to have the social willpower to stand together strong and confident.

In the next chapters, we will begin exploring the principles and sciences that form the basis of Axiogenics and its relevance to your life, your organization, and our world. From there, we will explore the practices that will bring the power of The Central Question alive in your world, your life, and your work.

• • •

CHAPTER
2

Value, Values, and Value Judgments

"In making judgments, the Early Kings were perfect, because
they made moral principles the starting point of all their
undertakings and the root of everything that was beneficial.
This principle, however, is something that persons of mediocre intellect
never grasp. Not grasping it, they lack awareness, and lacking awareness,
they pursue profit. But while they pursue profit, it is absolutely impossible
for them to be certain of attaining it."

~ *Lü Bu-wei 246 B.C., Chinese Prime Minister*

Values

Our "Values" may not be the real guiding force in our lives.

"The biology of the human brain is hard wired to add value."

~ George E. Pugh

Axiogenics is not about imposing or promoting any moral, religious, or ethical agenda, unless one views the idea of promoting a system for maximizing net value in the world as a moral or ethical agenda. If that's the case, then we proudly stand guilty as charged. That being said, it is important for us to explore the concepts of Values, value, and value judgments so that we draw meaningful distinctions between them.

"Values" (capital "V") refers to the ideals or principles we hold as important, such as honesty, integrity, excellence, quality, compassion, customer service, etc. Values come in two broad forms: Preferential Values (e.g., family, career, health, financial security, etc.) and Moral Values (e.g., honesty, fidelity, integrity, hard work, etc.). To a great degree, these basic human Values are engrained in our cultures and there is mounting evidence that certain "moral" Values may even be embedded in our DNA.

Unfortunately, in reality, our actions are not always consistent with our professed Values. How often do your preferential Values (i.e., family) conflict with your moral Values (hard work)? How often do you feel that you have to violate one in order to conform to the other?

For many people, Values are merely an expression of their *perception* of what they think ought to be important to them. Their Values are more like aspirations and intentions than actual thought processes that determine their daily decisions and actions.

Consider the workaholic who claims, "Nothing is more important than being a good parent," yet never has time for his kids. Or the retail store that espouses "customer services" as a core Value, yet, in the interest of lowering labor costs, never has enough people working the cash registers, resulting in long checkout lines.

Clearly, there is nothing wrong with having and promoting Values. Values can provide a kind of moral compass as well as a common bond between people, and cultures, and in teams. But, is there something deeper or more fundamental driving our choices and behaviors?

Yes. What really drives our choices, and even drives our Values, is our *perception of what creates value (little "v")*.

. . .

You Are Value-Driven

Your perception of what is of greatest or greater value in the moment drives your thoughts, choices, actions, and reactions.

"I conceive that the great part of the miseries of mankind are brought upon them by false estimates they have made of the value of things."

~ Ben Franklin

A meta-study of numerous disciplines in the fields of human and physical sciences (from neuroscience to social science, axiology to psychology, and anthropology to biology), suggests that value judgments are at the epicenter of all life activity—*value drives the mind-brain process.* [5] Put another way:

In any moment of choice,
conscious or even sub-conscious (habitual),
your perception of what will create the greatest net value,
will determine the choice you make.

We adopt our "Values," because we perceive, at some level, that they will add greater value to our life.

Virtually every conscious choice you have ever made has been an attempt to create greater value *from your perspective.* If you've ever snapped at or berated someone, it was because, in that moment, your mind-brain

---

[5] Nanschild, D. & Davis, H. 2007. The 'V' Factor: thinking about values as the epicentre of leadership, learning and life. 13th International Conference on Thinking. Norrkoping, Sweden.

determined that was the 'best" or "right" thing to do. If you have ever given someone a helping hand, it was because, in that moment, it seemed to be the thing that would create the most value. If you have ever made a mistake, taken a wrong turn, or acted in ways you later regretted, all that happened was that there was a gap between your *subjective perception* of what could create value and the *objective reality* of what would create value.

Many of us can have a difficult time differentiating between *objective* and *subjective* value. We *evalu*ate and make value judgments about something to determine what we *think* its value is. At that moment, the value we place on it occurs to *us* to be the actual (objective) value: You may say something's value *is X*. In truth, the value may be *X only to YOU* and may be quite different to someone else.

For example, could there be a difference, a gap, between the value you perceive in a task compared to the value your boss, employee, or a child perceives? *Subjectively*, any perspectives could be valid because the value *is* different for each person. However, the actual, *objective* value that the completed task creates in the world may be quite different from how any one person perceives it.

> "In many respects, we do not 'see' with our eyes;
> we 'see' with our values, our minds."
>
> ~ Dr. Leon Pomeroy[6]

When you make a value judgment, you are giving your own meaning to what you are valuing. In other words, the value you give something is based on the meaning you give it. That meaning, like tinted glasses, becomes the filter through which your subsequent perceptions take shape. This perception then becomes the basis for yet another value judgment, then another and another. So, people are driven by a cycle of perception-judgment-meaning, perception-judgment-*more*-meaning,

---

[6] (Pomeroy 2005, 38)

and so forth. Does this seem a bit like the chicken and the egg? It is, and it doesn't really matter.

What really matters is your capacity to make good and accurate value judgments. Three things determine the quality and accuracy of your value judgments:

1. Your capacity to *conceive* what would make something good or give it value.
2. Your capacity to *perceive* whether or not something has all the things/properties that would make it good.
3. Your capacity to *discern* the <u>relative</u> value of one thing compared to the value of another.

Notice how all three of the above capacities are about *subjective* processes (conceiving, perceiving, discerning). In Chapter 4, you will learn that only your *value judgments* are subjective. In reality:

*   There is an *objective* definition of what makes something good.
*   There is an *objective* reality as to whether or not something has what it needs to be good or valuable.
*   There is an *objective*, universal hierarchy that determines the relative value of everything.

Our *perception* of what creates or adds value is often inaccurate. Our perception is filtered through a complex web of thoughts, life-experiences, emotional memories, habits of mind, Values, previous assumptions, desires, fears, knowledge, priorities, and beliefs, and other sensory inputs. Most of these stimuli may never rise to the level of our consciousness, but they will have great influence on us nonetheless. Quite often, some of these are in conflict with each other, creating added stress.

There is an interesting game on the market called *Scruples*®. The game has players ask questions like:

'Your spouse has become a moody, nervous wreck since she began day trading on the Net. But she made $10K in a month. Do you ask her to stop?'

'The judging committee of a national high school science competition asks if you, the parent, are the one who actually did your child's winning science project. Your son has already claimed that he did it himself. The truth is, you did it. If you lie and claim that your son did the project, he wins the grand prize and a four-year scholarship. If you tell the truth, he loses. Do you admit the truth?'

If you ask people to decide which of two options is most important to them, such as kindness or honesty, making money or making friends, keeping the peace or standing up for what you believe, most people will respond, "It depends."

Certainly, in any given situation, it is appropriate to weigh the pros and cons of your options. The question really is will you consistently make choices in alignment with your Values or will you sometimes act in ways contrary to your Values?

When faced with a choice between family and career, one choice will be perceived, in any given moment, as having higher value than the other. Moreover, perception can change from moment to moment.

A man may do or say things around his buddies that he wouldn't dare say if his wife were present. It may be that around his buddies he values being liked, fitting in, being "cool" or admired and so he acts crudely. Then around his wife, so that she perceives him the way he wants her to perceive him, he acts very differently, hides his "alter-ego," or even claims to be offended by what his friends do or say.

How often do "loving" parents unwittingly behave or react in ways that seem mean, critical and disvaluing? How often have you justified bending or ignoring a rule out of expedience or by convincing yourself that it won't really hurt anyone else?

Think about it: in most cases, when you tell a "little white lie," justify a choice that is contrary to your "higher conscience," or adjust your

Values to "fit the situation," aren't you really making a self-centric, self-serving value judgment?

Imagine yourself in this situation: it's 5:30 PM and you promised (for the hundredth time) you would be home by 6 PM for the family dinner. However, you still have an hour's worth of work to do or your boss will be angry. You want to go home, but your job may be on the line. What you decide to do, even sub-consciously, will be determined by the value you place, *in that moment*, on the two options.

Say What?

Your mind may be screaming right now, "But, I don't have a choice! Staying at work doesn't mean I value my work more than my spouse!"

The truth is, you always have a choice. You may not like the consequences of one choice, but you do have a choice. Invariably, the need to make the choice between going home and staying at work (for example), is just the culmination of many choices that preceded the current situation. In this scenario, you might have chosen to work through lunch, made less phone calls, taken fewer breaks, or closed your office door so you wouldn't be disturbed and distracted throughout the day. There were many choices leading up to the "moment of truth." In the end, your choice will be value-driven, though perhaps skewed or dominated by the amazing power of the human mind for self-deception and justification.

How do you plan your day? Is it based on what you want to do, what you "need" to do, what is actually important to get done, or a combination of these? Perhaps you don't plan your day at all, preferring either to follow a well-established routine or simply to "take it as it comes." Whichever it is, it's based upon your priorities. Priorities are based on value judgments. The higher value (or potential value) you judge something (or the results of something) to have, the higher its priority.

Of course, value judgments weigh both the costs and the benefits of options. "High value" may be as much a function of potential loss as it is potential gain. For example, when something unexpected comes up, you have to decide whether or not dealing with the unexpected event is of higher value than your original plan: what if you do deal with it and what if you don't?

Most of this deliberation can occur below the level of consciousness when you are running on "auto-pilot." Consider the estimate that people have between 12,000 and 50,000 thoughts every day. The majority of those thoughts are sub-conscious and automatic (habitual) and are based on value judgments made in the past and converted into habits and perspectives. What's magnificent about your mind is that you have the power, in any moment, to make *conscious* choices, *independent* of your habits. However, the quality of your perceptions and your capacity to make good value judgments will still determine the quality of your choices. Moreover, your habitual value perceptions and habits may not always be supportive of your Values.

· · ·

No Neutral Choices/Actions

> Doing nothing, isn't nothing. Neutrality is a fallacy.

We would like to invite you to consider the possibility that every choice or action either adds or subtracts net value: *there is no neutral*. Even inaction is not neutral because inaction just keeps the status quo in place, and the status quo, itself, is either adding or subtracting value. The only time that inaction adds greater value is when any action you could take would reduce value: when the status quo is already creating the greatest net value. So, the essential question in any choice or decision is which choice adds the most value? Should you do something different, keep doing what you are doing, or do nothing at all? These are all, ultimately, value choices.

It makes sense that if you want to optimize value in your life, or in any situation, then you must maximize your capacity to recognize relevant gains and losses of value. You have to be able to compare options, choices, and actions and accurately determine which choice produce the greatest net (optimal) value. That's why The Central Question is so important.

$$\cdots$$

The Net-Net of Optimized Value

> *Net* value does not necessarily mean positive value for all people all the time. It's a question of balance.

To optimize means to create the best possible results under the circumstances. Obviously, not all choices can add value to all people all the time, not even valuegenic choices. Most situations in life require assessing value from multiple perspectives and then making a decision based on the sum total of all relevant positives and negatives.

Some decisions may seem to be good (adding value) for one person and bad (taking away value) for another. Take, for example, the decision of whether or not to fire an under-performing employee. Imagine this conversation going on inside the boss's head just after he asks himself The Central Question:

"On the surface, letting him go is the best thing for the company, but bad for the employee. Then again, maybe he will learn something from being fired, and that would be good. Intrinsically, people have more value than profits and productivity, so perhaps it would be wrong to fire him. But, he is very disruptive. Having him here is causing a lot of stress for the other workers and everyone's productivity is suffering. On the other hand, the guy has three young children and his wife is suffering from health issues. They really can't afford to lose their insurance and, without a job, he won't be able to pay the COBRA premiums. Still, I need someone in that position who can do the job or none of us will have a job. I know he's technically capable; he just doesn't seem to have the desire or motivation to do a good job. What's more, he seems to be unwilling to adopt our new initiatives to be a more valuegenic organization. Would letting him go suggest that we're not actually valuegenic at all? What do I do!?"

Personal mastery is about being able to take all these perspectives, know which are the most relevant and important, weigh the pluses and minuses appropriately and accurately, and then make the best possible choice you can to generate the greatest *net* value. This is the heart of The Central Question and the essence of being valuegenic: to optimize the value you generate to the best of your current ability. The more you develop your capacity, the more net value you can create and the greater success you can achieve. This is not always easy. However, it is always worthwhile.

. . .

Value Judgments

What drives a person's thoughts, reactions, and choices is their value judgments. Therefore, neither money nor love, but value judgments, are the root cause of good and evil.

"Your brain creates your reality. It is not what happens to you in life that determines how you feel; it's how your brain perceives reality that makes it so."

~ Daniel G. Amen

The verb 'valuing' is the act or process of placing a value on something. In other words, valuing is the process of making a *value judgment*. While you may think of valuing in concrete terms, such as giving something a value of $10, what you are really doing is valuing in *relative* terms. When you establish a price, for instance, you are valuing the item or service relative to the value you place on the dollar amount. For example, if I say I will sell you my car for $10,000, what I'm actually saying is that your $10,000 is worth as much or more to me than the car. If you feel that owning the car is worth equal to or more than your $10,000, then we'll make a deal. However, if you value my car less than your $10,000, we won't make a deal.

On one hand, wars are fought over value judgments: not just be-tween nations, but between people. On the other hand, love and com-passion are also driven by value judgments.

Value, and how you make value judgments, is much more complex than the above examples might suggest. What's more, because we often view things from multiple perspectives, the affect of our value judg-ments on our behaviors and choices can be equally complex.

For example, let's take a closer look at the process of valuing ideas. We have found that, for most people, the "quality" of their ideas is closely linked to their self-esteem. Imagine the internal conversation a person might have if they could slow down their mind, their habit-driven perspectives, perceptions, and their emotional reactions:

> *"What if they don't like my idea? How could they not? But, what if they think that my idea is not as good as theirs? That would mean they don't think I have as much to offer and maybe I'm not as good as they are. Or even worse, that could mean they don't like me! I have to find a way to make sure they see how good my idea is."*

If someone is not open to or does not like our idea, we may perceive (make it mean) that we are somehow "less than," or not good enough. We may feel misunderstood, unappreciated, or even disvalued. In such situations, we may find it hard to be open to the ideas of others and we can easily become defensive and even argumentative. It becomes per-sonal and often emotional. This can result in contentious relationships because no one wants to lose the argument, regardless of who actually has the best idea.

Interestingly, our research shows that emotional attachment to our own ideas, and/or a tendency to be resistant to other people's ideas, is present at some level in about 95% of all relationships. We are often feeling crushed by others, doing the crushing ourselves, or both.

Here's another example. In this scenario, a manager has been con-versing with a subordinate who has an idea for a "better way to do things." Based on the manager's knowledge and experience, clearly the idea is not a good one. Assuming it really isn't a good idea, what might happen in the mind of the manager? What concerns and issues might the manager be dealing with?

- Keeping people on task and productive
- Making good use of organizational resources to optimize results
- Having the employee feel valued
- Being distracted from his or her own work to listen to the idea
- Being concerned about what other people will think if a subordinate has a better idea than the manager
- Feeling fear of change and risk
- Having a need to rein in this "rogue" employee

How would you react or manage the situation?
- Would you look for value in the idea or even in the effort they put into trying to improve results?
- Would you value or disvalue the person with the idea?
- Would you want to "nip it in the bud" and refocus the person on the way it's "supposed" to be done?
- Would you become impatient?
- Would you try to understand why the person thinks there is something wrong with the current process?

How you would decide to handle this situation will be determined by the relative value you perceive (value judgments) on all the various issues involved—what's good for the company, for the employee, and for you.

The decision-making/value judging process can be highly complex. Before making a final decision your brain can go through a countless number of considerations, judgments, assumptions, calculation, possibilities, cross-references, and conclusions—any one of which may or may not be either accurate or even relevant. Much of this mental processing can happen automatically—and seemingly instantaneously—at the subconscious level: in the habit centers of the brain.

In his book, *Blink*[7], Malcolm Gladwell makes a compelling case that snap decisions or judgments are often better than well-thought, introspective ones. He poses the question, "Why do some people follow their instincts and win, while others end up stumbling into error?"

In part, the answer is simply that some people's instincts are better than others' are. But, as Gladwell shows, "instincts" can be greatly improved through trial and error, study, and practice. Additionally, he writes, "*Blink* reveals that great decision makers aren't those who process the most information or spend the most time deliberating, but those who have perfected the art of 'thin-slicing'—filtering the very few factors that matter from an overwhelming number of variables."

Gladwell posits that thin-slicing can be either a very good thing or a big mistake. Using a small amount of information to make generalized decisions can have highly detrimental results. However, a small amount of highly relevant information, combined with an innate capacity to discern the value of that information accurately, can be all that is required to make good decisions and act decisively.

For anyone who has read and enjoyed, *Blink*, take heart: Axiogenics can help you learn to "blink" better.

Whether you are "blinking" or thinking, your perceptions are filtered through your *personal value hierarchy*, or *value structure*.

• • •

---

[7] (Gladwell 2005)

Your Personal Value Structure

We all have a unique, personal value structure that, when we let it, runs our life and determines our future.

"The state of any individual's mind, as well as the state of his values, is the result of his experience during a long complex chain of past decisions."

~ George E. Pugh[8]

Your *Personal Value Structure* is forged from *how you perceive and interpret all of your life experiences.* As previously pointed out, as you go through life, you place a value on everything, which in turn becomes a filter through which you value other things and subsequent experiences. With every experience, and the meaning and value you give to that experience, your value structure changes a little. Sometimes it changes for better, sometimes for worse.

Your personal value structure is the relative, hierarchical order in which things have value to you: making friends vs. making money, for example, or quality time with family vs. productive time on a project.

All conflict (internal and external) is the result of conflicting value structures and perceptions. The conflict may be within our own value structure (internal) or between our value structure and another's (external).

Remember, people have as many as 50,000 thoughts each day and many of them relate to the valuing process. Have you ever had the experience of being in a situation and recognizing that from one perspective you were in agreement, but from another you were in conflict?

For example, a couple in New Jersey may agree that they want to spend a winter holiday with family, but disagree as to which family: her family that lives three hours away in New Hampshire, or his family that lives on the beach in Hawaii. Business partners may agree to cut back on expenses, but disagree on which expenses they should cut, such as marketing or research and development.

---

[8] (Pugh 1977)

Your value judgments influence both your conscious and sub-conscious thinking. Either way, the conclusions you make about the "right" thing to do may not always be accurate. How many times have you acted or reacted in some way, only to later realize that you had erred in your judgment? Clearly, our conclusions about the "right" thing are not always right.

Hindsight can sometimes be 20/20, but what if you could have 20/20 foresight? What if you could learn to catch yourself *before* you acted or reacted in an unproductive way? What if you could learn to shift to a different perspective, one in which you have greater clarity and wisdom, and then make a better choice? Taking it a step further, what if you could deliberately change your value structure such that your *first* thought was the one that held the greatest potential for optimum value generation? You can!

Ironically, what usually gets in the way of making really good choices with 20/20 foresight is that we are overly focused on our own desires, perceptions, and ideas.

• • •

From Self-centric to Valuegenic

> YOU are your biggest saboteur and your greatest asset.

> "A person starts to live when he can live outside himself."
>
> ~ Albert Einstein

Our culture, education, social pressures, and even the advertisements that bombard our psyche, tend to cultivate a materialistic, *self-centric* perspective on life. Unwittingly, we buy into constantly reinforced messages that overtly or covertly cause us to compare ourselves with each other or with a social "ideal." This creates habitual thought processes concerning our own needs, desires, expectations, and self-worth. These habits of mind tend to cause us to filter our value judgments through a membrane of self-concerns, such as:

"What's in it for me?"

"What will I get out of it?"

"How can I get what I want?"

"What will they think of me?"

"How can I win?"

"How can I look good?"

Notice that each of the above examples is self-centric. How often do you have these kinds of thoughts? When you focus primarily on self-concerns such as survival, control, avoidance, fear, winning, getting your needs fulfilled, being liked, etc., you are being self-centric.

Ironically, a self-centric mindset severely limits your ability to actually get more of what you want and less of what you don't. When we are self-centric, we tend to be over-focused on enhancing our own abundance at the expense of someone else's—even if we don't realize we're doing it. This mindset *will* eventually cause a net loss of value.

When you are being self-centric, your "central question" is likely to be something like: "What choice can I make and action can I take that serves me the most right now?" The self-centric "right" choice is whatever you think serves *you* the most. But this may well not be what actually optimizes net value, not even for you.

When you are *value*-centric, however, it's not all about you; it's about adding value, *period*. Your *intention* is to create the greatest possible net value for everybody, including yourself. The value-centric person, thinks in terms of The Central Question: "What choice can I make and action can I take, in this moment, to create the greatest net value?"

Taking it a step further, a value*genic* person doesn't just have an intention to create greater net value, they *actually* do create greater net value. Value-centric intentions are the starting point; valuegenic results are the goal. For most people there is a gap between the starting point and the goal. Learning to bridge that gap, is what The Central Question and Axiogenics are all about.

Remember, our Values may represent our ideals, beliefs, and intentions, but our thoughts and actions may not always be congruent with them. We are all masters at justifying our choices and actions. However, the truth is, except perhaps in some unique circumstances, when you are being self-centric your value judgments can easily go out of alignment with both your Values and what actually creates the greatest net value.

When you are truly being valuegenic, your Values and your value structure are not circumstantial, out-of-sync with each other, or self-centric. You are more likely to adhere to your Values because both your intentions and your value structure support you in creating the greatest net value, *no matter what role or circumstances* you are in. Your Values, then, are not merely who you *intend* to be, they are an expression of *who you really are!* When you are valuegenic, you have balance, congruence, and self-integrity—you optimize value in every area of your life.

While a self-centric view is more about *getting*, a valuegenic approach is more about *giving, cooperating, and co-creating*. This may sound like just another lovely idea and a nice, spiritually enlightened philosophy, however, these principles are found everywhere—from the symbiotic relationships between single-celled animals to highly functional businesses and organizations—because, life is about creating value.

Value is only optimized when we move away from a self-centric (I/me) view of the world to a valuegenic (we/us) approach to life; not just as individuals, but as organizations, families, and societies.

Eliminating "I", "Me", "My"

Try this little exercise. Select a period of time during the day, say an hour, when you will be interacting and conversing with other people. For that hour, follow these rules:

1- Drop the words, "I", "me", and "my" from your vocabulary.

2- Don't refer to yourself in the third person.

3- Communicate what is true for you and adds value in a way that makes sense.

Be very self-aware of what you are thinking and what you are about to say. If you "hear" any of these words ("I", "me", "my") in your head, take note that what you are thinking and what you are about to say may be more about you than what is truly most important. For example, if someone shares a good idea with you, the most likely response for many people is, "I think that's a good idea." This response inadvertently puts the focus on what YOU think about the idea. What you think about the idea may not be what matters most. What matters most is the goodness of the idea and acknowledging the person who had it.

A truly valuegenic response would simply be, "That's a good idea." Or, even better, "You have a really good idea there."

Obviously, there are times when it is appropriate to use "I", "me", or "my". For example, if someone directly asks you what you think about their idea, it may be appropriate to say, "I like your idea."

Here are a few more examples:

"I, Me, My" Focused	Valuegenic
I love you.	You are so loveable.
I liked that presentation.	That was a good presentation.
I need you to come here.	Could you come here?
Tell me how you are feeling.	How are you feeling?
I really enjoyed that.	That was really enjoyable.

This exercise, or game if you like, is designed to help you raise your self-awareness and to recognize how much of your thinking and speech has been about you. During the exercise, see if you can shift your thinking in such a way that it communicates even more powerfully and directly what really adds value, while not being about you at all.

Keep in mind, it's just an exercise; a game. Of course, you don't want to be rude. "How can I help you?" is still better than "What do you want?"

• • •

Value is the Driver of Change

We only change when we value the benefits of the change more than the benefits of the status quo.

> "If you want to move people, it has to be toward a vision that is positive for them, that taps important values, that gets them something they desire, it has to be presented in a compelling way, that they feel inspired to follow."
>
> ~ Dr. Martin Luther King

Change is hard for some people. If you value the potential benefits of a change more than the status quo, you are more likely to change. Conversely, if you value the status quo more than the value that a change could bring, you may resist change, perhaps even resent or sabotage attempts to force you to change. For example, until a smoker values their health more than smoking, they are unlikely to quit smoking.

It can be a challenge for many people to reconcile the known present with the unknown future that lies on the other side of change— "Better the Devil you know," as the saying goes. We may wonder, "What will it mean? Will I be ok?" In the face of the unknown, it's easy to imagine the worst, and the worst has very little value.

Perceived future value can also act as a powerful motivator. Have you ever known someone who is constantly making changes: changing jobs, coming up with a new scheme or business idea, thinking of the next best way to achieve something, get rich, or find "greener pastures"? Below every drive for change is a perception that the status quo is not creating enough value and that the "new idea" will.

What are the chances that the perceived value and/or perceived risk of a change are inaccurate—misperceived? Remember, the *process* of making value judgments is subjective. That is to say, a choice, action, or attribute might be *perceived* as either adding or subtracting value, regardless of whether or not it *actually* adds or subtracts value.

If you base your value perceptions on appropriate, high-VQ perspectives they will be more complete and accurate. Therefore, would it not be reasonable to project that you could also make good decisions regarding change using these same decision making capacities? Howeverer, if you attempt to make decisions from low-VQ perspectives, isn't it likely that the accuracy of your perceptions regarding change may also be diminished?

Most changes have elements of both perceived (added) value and perceived risk. Ultimately, one must weigh the relative value and the relative risks. The final choice (to change or not to change; to act or not to act) will be based on the net balance of the risks and rewards—the value that we perceive and place on each. The goal is to make sure your value perceptions are as accurate as you can make them.

Thanks to our ability to measure VQ, you can discover the unique perspectives by which *you* can best evaluate potential changes to improve your capacity to make good choices; and you don't need a high IQ to do it.

> "Everyone has inside of him a piece of good news. The good news is that you don't know how great you can be! How much you can love! What you can accomplish! And what your potential is!"
>
> ~ Anne Frank

• • •

VQ and Your Personal Value Structure

VQ is more important than IQ, EQ, or even "GQ."

Earlier you learned that VQ is the measure of your capacity to make good value judgments. You have also learned that you have a unique personal value structure that forms the basis of all your choices, actions, and reactions. Moreover, you've learned that your value structure and perceptions will influence your willingness to make changes. Bringing these concepts together, we can say that your VQ (Value-judgment intelligence Quotient) is an objective measure of how well your value structure can support you in making choices and changes that will maximize your success.

No matter how smart, sensitive, good-looking, or well-connected you are, real success can only be maximized if you can actually put these assets and resources to good use.

VQ Trumps IQ

The world has a great abundance of intelligent people who fail to live up to their potential. They make mistakes and misjudgments. While a person with high IQ may know a lot and be able to learn very quickly, a person with high VQ has tremendous perception. High-VQ people have a high capacity to make good choices about how to put knowledge to the best use; they can use greater intuition and empathy to connect with people, understand the nuances of net value, take highly-effective action, and more.

Research conducted by UCLA social neuroscientist, Matthew Lieberman, suggests that high-IQ people tend to be less self-aware than low-IQ people. Like IQ, however, VQ only matters if the person *applies* this talent by being valuegenic in their approach to life. It's not about having smarts, it's about having wisdom. Based on Lieberman's research, it seems that a high IQ could potentially interfere with a person's ability to increase either EQ or VQ, since self-awareness is a critical component to improving both.

VQ Trumps EQ

EQ (emotional intelligence) is a measure of empathy and social intelligence. EQ, like everything else, is value-driven. Therefore, EQ is actually a *subset* of VQ. A person can have a very high EQ, but still not make good decisions. A high EQ might help us make good choices about people, but it may not help very much when making good choices about a lot of other things.

Make no mistake, EQ is important. A high EQ requires a high level of empathy and compassion, a willingness to listen, and a fundamental recognition of the value in other people. EQ supports the concept that people are intrinsically of the highest value of all. Dr. Hartman demonstrated how net value and performance are always maximized when people think and act in ways that place the value of people at the highest level. He discovered that when employees feel intrinsically valued, they unleash an average of 40% more cooperation and productivity.[9] Conversely, when people do not feel intrinsically valued, they withhold 40% of their capacity for cooperation and productivity.

In the EQ world, the goal is to increase people's emotional and social intelligence (sensitivity). However, if a person's underlying value structure (in this case, the way they think about other people) doesn't support a higher EQ, it will be quite difficult for them to "change" unless their value structure changes.

Imagine if a person's value structure is such that they *genuinely* don't like dealing with people. In this situation, any effort to "act" more sensitive, despite their best efforts, may come off as insincere. Longterm, if their value structure (related to how they think about people) doesn't change, then acting sensitive and caring won't just *feel* insincere, it will *be* insincere.

VQ encompasses *all* of our thoughts, choices, and actions. Therefore, VQ is an indicator of the underlying value structures that drive EQ. By knowing one's VQ and applying axiogenic principles, we can improve EQ and all other performance factors; from procrastination to poor time/priority management, from low self-esteem to self-centeredness, and from fantasy and perfectionism to focus and follow-through.

EQ is important, but it is only one part of what it takes to succeed. Raise your VQ and you automatically raise your EQ.

VQ Trumps "GQ"[10]

It may seem that this is included only to poke a little fun at what seems to be a cultural preoccupation with "image." However, in reality, it

---

[9] (R. S. Hartman 1963)

[10] "GQ" comes from the monthly magazine originally called "Gentleman's Quarterly." It is a magazine about men's fashion and style. A "GQ" man is considered stylish and well groomed.

seems that about 70% of us do tend to overvalue the value of appearances.[11] People are easily impressed and sometimes even fooled by good looks, spiffy clothes, expensive cars, and other trappings of "looking good." Most people overvalue the value of appearances so much that they sub-consciously jump to conclusions about what appearances mean:

"He must be smart and successful. Look at how well he's dressed."
"She looks honest, I'm sure I can trust her."
"He looks hot. I'll bet he would make a great husband."
"She got good grades in school. She must be smart. Let's hire her."
"My nose isn't as pretty as hers, maybe I should get mine fixed."

The truth is, what you see is rarely what you get. A person with a high VQ is much more likely to have the capacity to see below the surface of appearances (i.e., to see the whole person), to not let appearances mean things they don't (e.g., that 'better looking' means 'better than' or 'better at'), and to make more accurate value judgments about others and themselves.

Good News, Bad News

The good news is that most people have a higher VQ and a greater capacity for being valuegenic than they actually use. For example, when they choose, most people can be more open and compassionate. They can be wiser in their choices about how they can create genuine value in their lives and in the lives of others. Value is the life-blood of success. We all have the ability to create more value and, therefore, more success.

The bad news is that over 90% of assessment subjects also show significant tendencies towards being self-centric. The issue is that our self-centric thoughts tend to dominate and interfere with our ability to accurately answer The Central Question and be valuegenic. Self-centric habits of mind are like lumps of cholesterol in an artery that restrict the

---

[11] Based on data from thousands of assessments.

natural flow, threaten our health, rob us of energy, and limit our natural abilities. Self-centric thinking restricts the life-blood of success.

By nature or by nurture, we all have some elements in our VQ profile that imprison our spirit, interfere with our strengths, and serve us poorly. They are our "weaknesses" and tend to promote self-centeredness. All of us also have elements in our VQ profile that hold the keys to greater levels of value-centeredness and higher capacities to create value in our lives. These are our strengths.

Your propensity for success is maximized when *both* your VQ (your capacity to make good value judgments) and your value-centeredness, (your intentional focus on creating value) are maximized.

The best news is that by applying the principles and practices of Axiogenics, you can learn to maximize the best in your VQ profile. You can reduce or even eliminate the negative effects (e.g., mediocrity, failure, stress, and suffering) that the worst in your VQ profile may have created in the past. You can free yourself from the self-imposed life-sentences of your perceived weaknesses and unleash more of the unlimited promise of your potential.

> Dr. "Charley," a chiropractor, was one of my coaching clients. The income from his practice was nowhere near where he wanted and, frankly, needed it to be.
>
> By assessing his VQ we discovered that he had a natural and brilliant, yet buried, ability to relate to people. The problem was that his self-respect was so low he was afraid to connect with people. He was immensely concerned about whether or not people liked him, and was so convinced that they wouldn't; that he came off very shy; mousey even. His fear kept him from venturing out into the community to promote his practice and he had a hard time talking to his prospective patients.

His breakthrough came when he realized that his practice wasn't really about him; it was about his patients and what chiropractic could do for them. This was a fundamental change in his perspective.

He began to focus his mind on using his strengths to relate to his patients, rather than allowing his lack of self-respect to make him fearful.

He became more involved in his community with a greater focus on service. He invited people to "come to the chiropractic clinic," rather than "come see me." This simple shift made a world of difference. In Dr. Charley's mind, he wasn't worth seeing, but chiropractic was well worthwhile, so he began to come from this perspective.

Can you guess what happened? More people started coming to his clinic. Patients began referring other patients. People felt that Dr. Charley really cared and that his practice was truly about them (not him); all because *he* began to see it that way.

Now here's the best part of his story. We re-assessed Dr. Charley after 4 months of coaching. His VQ for self-respect had improved dramatically. He reported that he felt like a new and different person. He felt confident, was enjoying his life, and people genuinely seemed to enjoy him. In those four months, his practice more than doubled. He even acknowledged that this change in his perspective saved his marriage.

With our coaching clients, we often conduct before and after assessments. What the data shows is that VQ scores improve by an average of 19% after our initial coaching process.

• • •

Making The Shift

> We don't have to beat our heads against the wall in an effort to fix ourselves, eliminate bad habits, or improve our performance. There *is* a much better way.

> "As human beings, our greatness lies not so much in being able to remake the world as in being able to remake ourselves."
>
> ~ Mahatma Gandhi

As you will learn in the next chapter, neuroscientists have discovered that trying to fix weaknesses is a red herring, a wild goose chase, a never-ending pursuit of an unachievable outcome. In fact, a substantial amount of what some of the bestselling "success gurus" have promoted is contrary to how we now know the brain works. This includes most behavior modification techniques, positive thinking, fantasizing, and even common gratitude practices.

If you've tried to break a bad habit, get other people to change their behaviors, or tried to fix yourself or others in any way, you know that it is extremely difficult. It usually takes a substantial amount time and effort, it's fraught with emotional stress, and rarely produces long-lasting results.

Unfortunately, the typical approach to "fixing weaknesses" forces us to try to use our weakness to fix our weaknesses. Not only is it a waste of the innate strengths we already have, it's a bit like putting the bank robber in charge of bank security.

As you now know, your value structure drives all of your thinking and your VQ profile measures the quality of your value structure. If you let your mind be driven by those elements of your VQ profile that can sabotage your success (your "weaknesses"), you're in for a tough time. But, you also have elements of your VQ profile that are supportive of your success. What if you could ensure that those elements, your strengths, are the ones that drive your thinking?

As you will soon discover, VQ is a critical piece of the puzzle pertaining to how you can leverage the way your brain *actually* works. Our brains are wired to add value. VQ is our capacity to see value. Measured or not, aware of it or not, VQ (our value perceptions) is the stimulus that causes changes in neuropathways of our brain.

By discovering your VQ and applying axiogenic principles, you can simultaneously:

1. Make maximum use of the strengths you *already* have to immediately create greater value, while transcending or even eliminating the negative impact of your sabotaging habits-of-mind ("weaknesses").

2. Use your mind to *deliberately* create additional neurological changes (new neurological pathways) that can cause your VQ—your capacity to make good value judgments—to measurably improve—thus, further increasing your potential for greater success.

"...and then the day came when the risk to remain tight in a bud was more painful than the risk it took to blossom."

~ Anais Nin

Later in the book, we'll tell you how you can take the VQ Profile Assessment for free so you can begin gaining the benefits even before you're finished reading!

• • •

CHAPTER
3

Neuroscience

"The brain gives the heart its sight.
The heart gives the brain its vision."

~ *Kall*

"If the human brain were so simple that we could understand it,
we would be so simple that we couldn't."

~ *Emerson M. Pugh*

Introduction

Neuroscience has shown us why many of the techniques for personal growth and development don't actually work very well.

"The brain is the organ of destiny. It holds within its humming mechanism secrets that will determine the future of the human race."

~ Wilder Penfield

Neuroscience is the science of how the brain works. Axiology is the science of value and, as you now know, value drives the processes of the mind-brain. To more fully understand how the two sciences relate, let's first explore some of the exciting discoveries in the field of neuroscience. This will set the stage for understanding how you can use Axiogenics to transform your life and your organization.

• • •

Neuroscience

The four-pound human brain is the most complex and powerful thing in the known universe.

Consider this: the brain has some 10 billion neurons. Each neuron has as many as 10,000 synaptic connections to other neurons. That alone amounts to more connections between your ears than there are known stars in the universe. More recently, neuroscientists have discovered that *glia* cells, long thought to be nonfunctioning cells, make up over 90% of the brain's structure; that's another trillion cells. What's more, glia cells may be every bit as involved in thinking and inner-brain communications as neurons and synapses.[12] Neuroscientist Andrew Koob, in his latest book, *The Root of Thought*, suggests that glia may be responsible for our "creative and imaginative existence as human beings."

The human brain is a highly social organ. According to Matthew Lieberman, a social neuroscience researcher at UCLA, "Most [of the]

---

[12] *Discover* magazine, September 2009, *The Brain*, by Carl Zimmer

processes operating in the background when your brain is at rest are involved in thinking about other people and yourself." It makes sense then, that the better we can understand how we think, the better decisions we can learn to make. The better we can make decisions, the more we can improve our own lives and the more we can contribute to the lives of others. In the end, isn't that what really matters in life?

• • •

Your Thoughts Are Not Who You Are

> You have thoughts, like you have a brain, but you are not your thoughts any more than you are your brain.

> "Your past is not your potential. In any hour you can choose to liberate the future."
>
> ~ Marilyn Ferguson

Neurologically, thoughts show up as biological phenomenon created through the firing of synapses in your brain. These synapses—trillions of them chained together into neuropathways that hold data, memories, impressions, habits of mind, and thought processes—are primarily the result of your conscious and sub-conscious life experiences.

What you think determines *how* you behave, *where* you go, *what* you attract to your life, *what* your life is about, *how* you feel, *when* and *why* you do what you do, and even what you will become. Your thoughts also determine the value you are able to perceive and create in the world, and ultimately, the quality of your life.

On one hand, you are not your thoughts you simply have thoughts. On the other hand, how often do your thoughts have you? How often are you "running on automatic," impulsively doing whatever comes to mind? For many people, the answer is "most of the time."

You have thoughts, just as you have a head and a stomach, and sometimes, hiccups, but YOU are not your head, your stomach, or your hiccups. Notice that you are having thoughts right now as you read this. Notice that you can actually observe yourself thinking. Clearly, you have the power to deliberately go beyond your thoughts and observe them as separate from yourself; you can separate your "self" from your thoughts. You can even observe yourself observing yourself. From the position of the "observer," you can judge if a thought is a good one or not, and whether or not it will add value. From here, you have the power to choose. You have the power to change!

So you *have* thoughts; you *have* ideals, Values, dreams, and goals. However, these are really more a reflection of the *perspectives* from which you see things. They are the filters through which you judge and discern everything in your life, including your thoughts about your thoughts, and about where you are going, what you should do, and why.

Just as you are not your thoughts, other people are not their thoughts either. How other people present themselves through their thoughts, actions, and behaviors is simply an outward expression of *where* they are, not necessarily *who* they are, or *what* their potential is.

Your perspectives on life, yourself, and the world naturally change as you mature, gain more experience, and go through stages in your life. Yet you can also consciously choose to change your perspective. In fact, you do it every day. Every decision-making process is a process of weighing options from various perspectives, and each of these perspectives uses a different set of thoughts.

Is there something more to thoughts than mere brain chemistry? We believe there is. The human spirit is something far beyond mere chemistry, neurons, and synapses. Our bodies and brains may be physical, but we believe there is something meta-physical (beyond physical) about us too; a higher-consciousness, a power or dimension that seems to connect us with something beyond our biological bodies. Is there some force in the universe or a cosmic system that science has not yet identified that causes us and everything in the universe to grow and expand? Is it God or some ethereal energy that gives us the power to see and the desire, to care about the differences between right and wrong, good and evil, adding value and taking value away? Whatever it is, there is something, and it's our connection with that something, that gives humankind our uniqueness in the known universe.

Still, we are biological beings. Somehow, in some fashion, our physical biology is intertwined with this seemingly meta-physical force. In his book, *The Biological Origin of Human Values*, George E. Pugh writes, "The biology of the human brain is hard wired to add value. Throughout the millennia of evolution, our brains have developed finely-tuned systems for quickly making value judgments about environmental stimuli to optimize our chances of survival."[13]

If this is so, how can we learn to use this phenomenon to our advantage? What if there is an objective framework and a science-based process for deliberately choosing to shift and improve one's capacity to think better; to perceive better, and to make better choices about what is right and wrong, what is good and what is evil, what adds value and what subtracts value? Not just so we can survive, but so we can thrive.

There is, and it's what you are learning about right now.

• • •

Neuroplasticity

The brain is constantly changing, unlearning and learning. YOU have the power to make it change the way you want it to change.

"Every man can, if he so desires, become the sculptor of his own brain."

~ Neuroscientist, Santiago Ramon y Cajal

In recent years, there has been an abundance of groundbreaking research in an area of neuroscience called *neuroplasticity*. Dozens of new books and articles on the subject come out each year, many of them in the mainstream press.

---

[13] (Pugh 1977)

Neuroplasticity is the brain's ability to reorganize itself, at any age, by forming new neural connections in response to life experiences, injury, or disease.

For example, in severe cases of epilepsy, surgeons can remove an entire hemisphere of the brain and, with time and therapy, the remaining hemisphere will take over the functions of the removed half.[14]

It was once believed that as we age, the brain's neuronal networks became fixed. The prevailing view was that our personality and ways of thinking were fixed around the age of seven. In recent years, however, new research has revealed that the brain never stops changing and adjusting, and that even personality can change and be changed. In fact, important brain functions integral to growth and change, actually improve with age.

Barbara Strauch, in her recent book, *The Secret Life of the Grown-Up Brain*, reports on a 50-year study of the cognitive abilities of the human brain as it ages: "What the researchers found is astounding. During the span of time that constitutes the modern middle age—roughly age forty through the sixties—the people in the study did better on tests of the most important and complex cognitive skills than the same group of people had when they were in their twenties. In four out of six of the categories tested—vocabulary, verbal memory, spatial orientation, and, perhaps most heartening of all, inductive reasoning—people performed best, on average, between the ages of forty to sixty-five."[15]

This increased cognitive ability is an improvement in precisely the kind of thinking that supports the process of shifting perspectives and making new synaptic connections. So, not only can we teach "old dogs" new tricks, it turns out "old dogs" may actually be better at learning them.

As a result of these discoveries, a substantial paradigm shift is now under way. Canadian psychiatrist, neuroscience researcher, and author,

---

[14] (Zimmer, The Brain 2009)
[15] (Strauch 2010)

Norman Doidge, states that he believes neuroplasticity is one of the most extraordinary discoveries of the twentieth century. It is his conviction (and ours as well) that this represents one of the single most important developments in brain science in hundreds of years.[16]

Research in the field of neuroplasticity has primarily been focused on helping patients overcome brain injury and/or disease by teaching them to "re-program" specific regions of the brain. As a result, neuroscience is giving hope, freedom, and new life to people who were once discarded by a world that either didn't care or didn't know how to help.

What's most relevant to our purposes, however, is how neuroplasticity offers new possibility and freedom to *anyone* who wants to make changes in how their mind-brain works to create a better life for themselves. In other words, how neuroplasticity applies to personal growth and development. Specifically, we can use the mechanics of neuroplasticity to consciously and deliberately change our minds. We can eliminate old habits of thinking that limit our success, and create new habits that propel our success.

Some of these discoveries will cause consternation for people who have been indoctrinated into certain long-held beliefs and approaches to personal and organizational development and training.

Neuroscience has revealed that many popular techniques for eliminating "bad" mental habits and creating new behaviors are *incongruent with how the mind actually works*. For example, as you will learn in the next sections, positive thinking may not be all that positive.

What follows is a basic exploration of what neuroscience teaches us about what doesn't work, what does work, and why. Let's start with a discussion about habits. By understanding the mechanics of how habits are formed and *how they can be eliminated*, we are better equipped to deliberately change our habits of mind.

• • •

---

[16] (Doidge, 2007)

Habits of Mind

> Habits of mind, it turns out, are much easier to change than we ever thought possible. We've just been going about it the wrong way.

> *"If I must be a slave to habits, let me be a slave to good habits."*
>
> ~ Og Mandino

The human brain has a strong preference for conserving energy and resources. Subconscious habits use much less energy and preserve conscious "processing" power for other purposes. In fact, generally speaking, the conscious mind cannot actually multitask, but the subconscious mind can. By creating habits, the brain improves efficiency. We depend upon habits to manage many aspects of life automatically.

Take driving a car, for example. When you first learn to drive a car, it requires tremendous mental energy. There is a lot that the mind must pay attention to: the speedometer, staying in one lane, using turn signals, observing road signs and signals, noting the position of other cars, etc. At first, you don't actually do all this at the same time; you simply shift your conscious attention from one thing to the other very rapidly. With enough repetition, your mind relegates some of these activities to the sub-conscious habit center of the brain. At some point, when you see a red light, you automatically brake and slow down with very little conscious thought. The brain actually sees the red light (hopefully) as an "error," which instantly, and often sub-consciously, causes the appropriate conditioned habitual response.[17]

Most mental habits develop through long-term, repetitive processes. However, not all habits are helpful in the end. For example, when life circumstances or people in our environments consistently give us the idea that we're not "good enough", our brain will eventually convert the conscious thought, "I'm not good enough," into a sub-conscious mental habit where it becomes a filter or perspective by which the person

---

[17] (Frida E. Polli 2009)

perceives themselves and the world. Quite literally, these mental habits are "programmed" into our brains as a set of neuropathways and synaptic connections that "hold" the thought pattern.

Generally, people think of negative habits, behaviors, and personality traits as "weaknesses." Some examples include: procrastination and pessimism; a weakness for food, sugar, or caffeine; disorganization and sloppiness; too much of a dreamer or not enough drive; shyness, selfishness, laziness, irresponsibility, impatience, irritability, (and the list could go on and on).

For centuries, many people have believed that habits of mind and "personality traits" are permanent and cannot be changed or eliminated; only tolerated and overcome through compensation. Still, people have tried. Typical approaches to "fixing" bad habits and negative thinking have focused on changing behaviors, developing new habits through brute-force repetition of behaviors and affirmations, or simply managing, tolerating, and compensating for the "weaknesses." Generally, these approaches are only minimally effective.

One of the most common methods for "fixing" bad or negative thinking and behavior is to compensate for it by affirming ("thinking positive") or forcing ("fake it till you make it" or "feel the pain and do it anyway") the desired thinking or behavior. This approach is deeply engrained in our culture. The problem is that the brain doesn't work that way, which is the reason why such a practice rarely produces genuine and lasting change.

We now know that we can deliberately change habits of mind through the mechanics of neuroplasticity. As it turns out, knowing your VQ is one of the keys to unlocking the power of neuroplasticity.

• • •

The Fiction of Fixing

> Fixing, compensating, and positive thinking rarely work. In fact, they can often cause more harm than good.

Most people are familiar with the long-promoted idea of deliberately thinking a desired thought often enough for the brain to turn it into a habit. Countless books and "success gurus" have touted this approach for centuries. Unfortunately, research in neuroscience has shown that it's just not that simple. In fact, this approach may be doing more harm than good.

Take "positive thinking," for example. One aspect of being human is our capacity to observe (be aware of) our own thoughts as they occur. We have the unique ability to "hear" our own thoughts—to catch ourselves thinking negative thoughts like:

- "I'm not good enough."
- "I can't do this."
- "It will never happen."

A common teaching by many is that when we find ourselves thinking a negative thought, we should compensate for the negative by thinking or affirming the opposite, something positive. For example, if I catch my mind thinking, "I'm not good enough," I should immediately tell myself, "I'm great." By doing this often enough, the "experts" suggest, that I'll create a new, more positive habit.

Unfortunately, all that actually happens is that we develop a habit of compensating for negative habit with what is little more than intentional self-deception. This approach is a bit like painting over rotten wood. Someday, the paint will chip off, exposing the raw, underlying original habit, only this time with potentially dire consequences, as it almost did for "Stan."

"Stan" had been highly successful in his 25-year career and attributed his success to his "positive mental attitude (PMA)." But his marriage had fallen apart. The divorce was very messy and resulted in bankruptcy, the loss of his home, his car, and his business. With no money, and no apparent prospects for making money, he was destitute and desperate; but he had a plan.

Thankfully, before he carried out his plan, he decided to check his email hoping for some kind of miracle that would save him. That "miracle" turned out to be an email I had sent to him, asking him to call me to discuss the "VQ" assessment report he had taken a few days earlier. Though we had never spoken before, something inside him urged him to pick up the phone and call. He did.

Within minutes, he admitted to me that he was on the verge of suicide. That very morning he had planned out what he would do and had begun "making arrangements." Despite his longtime practice of PMA, his VQ for self-esteem and a few other measurements were very low.

I asked him what was motivating him to give up. His answer was this: "Not only did I fail in my marriage, and now my business, everything I ever believed about success and motivation turned out to be a lie. Everything I had been telling myself about myself has been a lie. Now I know the truth; that I am a worthless human being and I don't want to live with that."

'Get him to call a suicide crisis helpline,' was my first thought, but my intuition told me that if I "rejected" him now, he would carry out his intentions. He had reached out to me in one last, fleeting spark of hope: I couldn't and wouldn't reject him.

To be continued . . .

Like many people, Stan had been a devout practitioner of "Positive Thinking" or "Positive Mental Attitude (PMA)." But, let's look closer at PMA from a neurological perspective.

Paraphrasing Hebb's Rule, a theory that neuroscientists often cite, "What's wired together, fires together." When you compensate for one thought by thinking a different thought, you create a connection, a kind of temporary synaptic pathway, between the two thoughts. Neuropathways work much the same as electrical circuits. When you energize one end of the circuit, it almost immediately energizes the other a well.[18]

Because of this principle, if you've been a practitioner of PMA, there is a good chance that when you tell yourself "I'm great" to compensate for a negative, you "hear" this little voice in your head saying something like 'No you're not. Who are you trying to kid?' What's happened is that the brain has "wired" (associated) the positive conscious thought to the old negative habit.

Moreover, the brain interprets your 'firing' of the negative thought as an indicator that you still need it. Therefore, the brain continues to preserve the old habit. Quite literally, rather than fixing the problem, you may end up *fixated* on the problem. Inadvertently, you end up doing even more battle with yourself—battles that you can't win by taking the fixing and compensating approach.

We want to make it clear that there are times when adopting a positive attitude or using affirmations can be beneficial. They can, for example, provide an extra measure of motivation, confidence, or the adrenaline or testosterone rush that is needed to take an action or accomplish a task. Professional athletes, performers, public speakers, and even sales people often use this technique to psyche themselves up before an event. When used to compensate for a weakness, however, compensating affirmations and positive self-talk provide little or no long-term benefit; you'll just have to keep battling the weakness, over and over again.

Breaking old habits through brute force is extremely difficult and often painful. It takes a huge amount of mental stamina, focus, awareness, determination, and willpower. Still, it's the only way most people

---

[18] (Lipton 2009, 97)

know, so they try, and try again. All too often, however, though convinced of their success, they are in fact, in a form of temporary self-deception. At some point, the old habit, which the mind has continued to preserve, will likely reactivate, triggered by difficult life experiences. When the "self-deception" is finally exposed, it can potentially have a catastrophic impact on the person.

As Dr. Bruce Lipton writes, in *Biology of Belief,* "The mere thinking of positive thoughts will not necessarily have any impact on our lives at all! In fact, sometimes people who 'flunk' positive thinking become more debilitated because they now think their situation is hopeless. The idea that we can compensate for negative thoughts by thinking positive is little more than a feel-good fiction of our hope and imagination."

Now back to Stan . . .

I didn't tell him that he was great. I didn't tell him that he was wrong. I listened to his pain and mined his VQ assessment for the source of his perceptions. It was very clear. I had him look at his assessment report and walked him through a few key points: first at the source of his struggles and then at the source of his strengths. I also explained some of the very things that you are reading about now. Suddenly he began to see how he had gotten to where he was (self-deception), and that all he had to do was use his considerable strengths to start making some immediate and important positive changes.

The next time we spoke, Stan began telling me about some of the amazing new things that had already started to happen in his life. Filled with a genuine enthusiasm he had not known in a very long time, he was making real progress toward creating a new life for himself.

• • •

Synaptic Pruning and Mental Re-tuning

You can make your weaknesses weaker by focusing on your true strengths.

It is said that a chain is only as strong as its weakest link. When we try to fix or compensate for our weaknesses, we are inadvertently adding our weakness to our chain of thinking.

Imagine, though, if you could create a new "good" thought *without* it being a compensation or connected in any way to an old "bad" habit? Furthermore, what if you could actually eliminate the synaptic connections that fire-up the negative habits and thoughts. Could you create a stronger, more helpful chain?

Through a process called *"synaptic pruning,"* neurological connections that are no longer used are allowed to atrophy (weaken) and fade away. While the brain is like a collection of electrical circuits, it is also like a muscle. When you repetitively flex a muscle, the body reinforces and may even strengthen the muscle. When you stop using a muscle for a prolonged period, the body stops supporting the muscle; it gets weaker and atrophies. Through synaptic pruning, our brain treats neuropathways in much the same way.[19]

Focus on What's Strong, Not What's Wrong

Using synaptic pruning to eliminate old thought patterns is not as difficult as it might seem. The solution is to "tune in" to an already existing genuine strength that can support a desired "good" habit independent of any "bad" habit. In this way, the new "good" neuropathway is created and nurtured without any connection or negative influence from the old "bad" habit. The more you nurture the new thought, the stronger it becomes.

We gave an example earlier about compensating for a negative thought, such as "I'm not good enough," by forcing yourself to think a

---

[19] (Woods and Zito 2009)

positive one, such as "I'm Great!" We then explained why that approach doesn't work. So, what can you do instead?

**Find a different perspective on the situation
that renders the idea, "I'm not good enough," irrelevant.**

The thought, "I'm not good enough," is a response to some situation or challenge. There is usually more to the thought than just "not good enough." More often, it takes the form of, "I'm not good enough *to be/do/have* ____ [something]." Let's assume that you have this recurring thought, "I'm not good enough to complete that task." Imagine also that, we've assessed your strengths and determined that you're actually very good at figuring out how to get things done *when you put your mind to it*.

If you can shift your mindset from questioning whether or not you're "good enough" to asking yourself how to get the task done, you'll be able to tap into your strength. In terms of what will create the greatest net value, the only thing that is relevant is your high ability to figure out how to get the task done. The false idea that you're not good enough to complete the task is simply irrelevant. Because it is irrelevant, when you are coming from your strength, it has no power. Through synaptic pruning, the more irrelevant an old habit becomes, the more it goes away.

Choose It and Fuse It

If you think about it, a "weakness" is, by definition, a strength you don't have. It's pretty hard to do anything with something you don't have. By "tuning in" you your genuine strengths, you render your weaknesses irrelevant. We all have strengths that we can apply to almost any situation if we know how.

Let's look again at the above scenario, this time from a different perspective. Remember, in this scenario, you actually do have the ability to get things done *when you put your mind to it*. What does it mean to "put your mind to it?" It means that you deliberately stay focused on using your strengths to complete the task. The task is not about you; and whether or not you think you're good enough *is irrelevant*.

By choosing to focus on your strengths, three things will begin to happen:

1. Through synaptic pruning, your weaknesses become weaker; they lose their power.
2. Through neuroplasticity, your strengths become stronger; they become the basis of new habits
3. Through action, you will perform better, create greater value, and provide yourself with evidence that you *can* learn and do things beyond your previous limits; you grow.

As you gather this new evidence of your true abilities, what do you think will happen to any low-self-image issues? What will happen to your self-confidence and your ability to see new possibilities for your future?

· · ·

Attention Density Develops Propensity (Habits)

> Deliberate change requires frequent conscious effort, attentiveness, and repetition over time.

It takes time, persistence, and consistent mindful attention to make permanent changes in habitual thinking. Neuroscientists call the frequency and intensity with which a person consciously practices a new way of thinking, *attention density*. It's like sanding and polishing a rough-hewn piece of lumber. To bring out the beauty in the unique texture of the grain, you have to sand in the same direction as the grain and the natural texture of the wood. It takes work and consistent focus over time, but the result is well worth the effort. Your mind works the same way.

By repeatedly going "with the grain" (paying attention to and using a genuine strength), rather than going against the grain (compensating for a bad habit), the neuropathways of a new habit start to take shape in the brain's habit center. With repetition, the neuropathways are "polished" and become more defined. In time, it takes less and less conscious mental energy to sustain the new thought pattern. Eventually, it will become a thing of beauty: a positive, "permanent" sub-conscious habit of mind.

Seminars, weekend retreats, and training programs are fine for teaching technical skills and imparting specific knowledge. Behavior and accountability-focused training and coaching can certainly help get and keep people on track. However, without targeting the underlying value structures that drive behavior, and without providing sufficient opportunities for practice and repetition over time, long-lasting changes are rare. All too often, people either become dependent on the support of coaching to stay "on-point" or they try to go it alone and revert to old ways of thinking once the coaching or training has ended.

• • •

Celebrate Successes!

> Celebration is more than just a nice feeling; it is an essential part of the neurological process of change.

Celebration is a powerful reinforcement of successes both large and small. Celebrating causes the brain to produce neuropeptides, such as dopamine, which is crucial in the development and "hardening" of the new neuropathways and synapses—the building blocks of mental habits.

To authentically celebrate an accomplishment or result requires that you recognize and acknowledge the value that the accomplishment or result created. Remember, value perceptions drive thinking. The more value you create, and the more you celebrate the creation of that value, the faster and easier new habits become sustainable.[20]

---

[20] (David and Vouimba 2009)

For this reason, it is important that people who are engaged in a process of change acknowledge themselves and receive acknowledgement from fellow stakeholders (family, peers, supervisors, and even employees) for the progress they are making. It's not just a nice thing to do; it's an essential part of the neurological process of change.

• • •

Amygdala Hijacks

> During an amygdala hijack, we have little possibility of thinking effectively about what we value or how we might truly add greater value.

One of the biggest situational challenges to having the presence of mind to even ask yourself The Central Question, let alone answer it, is what neuroscientists call an *amygdala hijack*.

The term 'amygdala hijack' was popularized by Daniel Goleman in his book, *Emotional Intelligence*. It describes what happens when a part of the brain called the amygdala "takes over" and, as a result, we react in ways that we may later regret.

The amygdala is a section of the brain that controls the emotions and the "fight or flight" response. Its job is to protect us from threats and to analyze input/stimuli using emotional memories. An amygdala hijack is marked by an over-response to a threatening situation in relationship to the magnitude of the actual threat. Examples include, snapping at someone "for no apparent reason" or becoming overly defensive and/or aggressive against a minimal or nonexistent threat. The amygdala does not necessarily know the difference between an actual and an imagined threat.

Your physical and/or emotional reactions are the same whether the threat is real or imagined. The physiological response is the result of a sudden rush of cortisol, adrenaline, norepinephrine, and other ligands and neuropeptides. It induces the very kind of instantaneous response that a terrorist attack creates when "normalcy" is interrupted by an unexpected horror. However, these threats need not be physical threats; they can be threats to your self-esteem, your authority, your control, your emotional well-being, or even your perception of reality.

When an amygdala hijack happens, we go "out of our [conscious] mind." The amygdala temporarily takes over and the neocortex (the thinking part of the brain) has virtually no chance to apply logic, reasoning, or intelligence to the situation. An amygdala hijack also affects the anterior cingulate cortex, the area of the brain involved in emotional control (resulting in less control). Typical effects of an amygdala hijack are shortness of breath, increased heart rate, and a tightening of muscles, including facial muscles. Even our voice can change no matter how much we try to "remain calm." A "hijack" may only last a few seconds or minutes, but the adrenaline rush will remain present and active for 18 minutes or so, while other neuropeptides can take hours to dissipate. The longer the amygdala hijack lasts, the longer it takes to calm down. As long as those neuropeptides are coursing through our bodies, we can't be our best. Spend an hour in an active amygdala hijack and you're likely to waste the entire day!

Compounding the problem, while cortisol stimulates the amygdala it also suppresses the hippocampus. The hippocampus is located right next to the amygdala. It is a sort of gatekeeper between the pre-frontal cortex, where conscious "working-memory" resides, and the long-term storage areas of the brain. This means that during an amygdala hijack we don't have access to the rational part of our brain. Have you ever been in a heated or stressful situation and, as much as you try, you can't remember some piece of important information, then, minutes or hours later, you remember? We commonly refer to this phenomenon as a "brain freeze." In a sense, that's exactly what's happening to parts of our brain during an amygdala hijack.

Not only is our ability to remember impaired during a hijack, but so is our ability to take in and interpret new information. We get "tunnel vision" and loose our awareness of other things going on around us. Have you ever had an emotionally charged argument with someone and then later were unable to clearly remember who said what? The interesting thing is that neither of you may be accurate in your memory of what actually happened, no matter how "certain" each of you feels.

What do value structures have to do with amygdala hijacks? Lots! It turns out that an increased capacity to see things accurately from multiple perspectives substantially reduces the risk and intensity of the emotional response that amygdala hijacks can create.[21] In addition, misperceptions of the nature of the "threat," caused by inaccurate perceptions and value judgments, often trigger the hijack. Sometimes we are quite conscious of what's happening and we *think* we're doing the "right" thing. Other times, the hijack can be instantaneous with little or no conscious awareness until it's too late.

During an amygdala hijack, we have little possibility of thinking effectively about what we value or how we might truly add greater value. In moments like this, we tend to lash out at people, at the world, at God, or even at ourselves. In an instant, we can violate our own Values.

During and immediately following an amygdala hijack, our emotions are "out of control" —not unlike a panic attack — and we temporarily lose a significant portion of our mental capacity to access memory or to process new information.

However, you can learn to approach conflict and stress from a more valuegenic perspective and potentially prevent an amygdala hijack before it drives you *and everyone around you* out of your minds. With a little self-awareness and sufficient self-discipline, you can simply ask yourself The Central Question. Try it today and see if it doesn't make a difference in how you react. You might not come up with the ideal answer, but you'll certainly be in a better frame of mind.

• • •

---

[21] (St. Jacques, Delcos and Cabeza 2010)

Stress–The Value Killer

Stress kills. Stress is optional!

Our coaching clients have reported that one of the most significant benefits of the work has been the reduction of their negative stress.

Where does stress come from? Based on what you've learned so far, especially the fact that value drives the mind-brain processes, can you see that a lot of stress is caused by gaps (differences) between our value expectations and our value perceptions? Psychologists distinguish stress in three ways: physical, emotional, and cognitive (mental).

Physical stress is stress on the body. Physical exertion and environmental stressors, such as pollution, chemicals, dehydration, and unhealthy foods cause physical stress.

Emotional and cognitive stresses originate in the mind-brain. More and more, scientists are discovering that both emotional and cognitive stresses can lead to severe, debilitating physical stress within the body. During an amygdala hijack, for example, the body experiences a flood of "stress-induced" neuropeptides, such as cortisol.

Small amounts of cortisol can be beneficial, resulting in a quick burst of energy, heightened memory function, a momentary increase in immunity, or reduced pain sensitivity. However, prolonged or frequent floods of cortisol can be highly toxic. Here are just a few of the detrimental effects of excessive cortisol:

- Impaired cognitive performance
- Suppressed thyroid function
- Decreased bone density
- Decreased muscle tissue
- Higher blood pressure
- Lowered immunity and inflammatory responses in the body
- Slowed wound healing, and other health consequences
- Blood sugar imbalances such as hyperglycemia
- Increased risk of heart attack and stroke

It gets worse. This is just what excessive cortisol can do; there are many other neuropeptides at work, which may have equally troublesome effects when we are under constant stress. These physiological responses occur in various combinations in all three forms of stress. Emotional and cognitive stresses usually lead to physical stress. However, the reverse is not always the case: physical labor or playing sports does not necessarily lead to cognitive or emotional stress.

Here's the kicker: contrary to what many scientists claim, *stress is optional.* By this we mean you have options. Stress is a matter of perspective and perception. You have the power to choose your perspective, but not always your perception.

When people are emotionally or cognitively stressed, they are usually looking at things from a perspective that has a low VQ and, therefore, their perceptive abilities are limited. They are stuck in a state of what cognitive therapists call *cognitive distortion*:

- All-or-nothing thinking (systemic)
- Overgeneralization
- Mental filtering (seeing what you want/expect to see)
- Disqualifying positive things as anomalies
- Over-focusing on the negative
- Jumping to conclusions
- Catastrophizing
- Emotional rationalization
  ("It's wrong because it upsets me.")
- Unreasonable/unrealistic expectations and "shoulds"
  (even if it doesn't look/feel unrealistic or unreasonable)
- Labeling and mislabeling self and others
- Blame, non-accountability, deflection

As you learned from the section on amygdala hijacks, under these conditions, we also have less access to our memory and reasoning abilities. We can easily suffer from tunnel vision, resulting in extreme action at one end of the spectrum and a deer-in-the-headlights (choking/paralysis) syndrome at the other.

Conversely, when people can bring a wider perspective to situations (e.g., be more valuegenic), they are more rational and experience less emotional and cognitive stress.[21]

Emotional and cognitive stress can also be created when using the compensation/fix-what's-broken/positive thinking approach to personal improvement. Quite often, this technique creates a dissonance or conflict between two mental perspectives—the old habit and the compensating affirmation. While this approach may help someone succeed in some area of their life, quite often, it's at the expense of another area of their life, (i.e., relationships, happiness, health, work, family, fun). Is it really worth it?

Because emotional and cognitive stress causes physical stress, learning to prevent emotional and cognitive stress is good for your health. Moreover, by reducing emotional and cognitive stress (which inhibit rational thought and cognitive abilities) you can also increase your overall performance.

Some would claim that they are at their best when they are under stress or pressure. We contend, however, that the "pressure" simply causes them to do something instead of nothing. Under stress, their "best" is only as good as the best they have learned to be. It's not the best they *could* be if they understood and practiced axiogenic principles.

For many people the very idea, let alone the process, of learning something new can be stressful. New learning often goes "against the grain" of old thinking. Learning suggests change and, as we've already discussed, some people have an aversion to change. But, if you're going to learn, change, or grow, you might as well go about it in the most effective, stress-free way you can.

Neuroscientists have identified a way of learning that nearly all elite performers use to *become* elite performers, it's called *deliberate practice*. Performance coaches use this approach because it produces the fastest, most reliable results. In addition to minimizing stress, it maximizes results by making use of neuroplasticity to accelerate the learning process.

· · ·

Deliberate Practice

Ah-ha moments are magnificent, but deliberate practice is what creates predictable personal mastery.

Lots of people have the good intention to grow and improve. However, good intentions, like goals, only have value when they are matched with effective actions and valuable experiences.

Occasionally, the "action/experience" required for learning seems to happen *to* us, without any conscious intention on our part. Many people have experienced at least a few intense "ah-ha" moments of enlightenment in their lives. Instantaneous "awakenings" are powerful, but they are also rather rare and unpredictable. Usually they are accompanied by very high levels of feel-good positive neuropeptides, such as dopamine and norepinephrine, that instantaneously create entirely new "permanent" thought patterns in the brain.

We're going to assume, since you are reading this book, that you like to be proactive in your personal growth rather than just waiting around hoping for a bolt of enlightenment to hit you. Instead of leaving it to chance and "good intentions," you prefer to be more deliberate.

Deliberate practice is not the same as ordinary practice. Practice is often rote repetition with very little focused thought, while *deliberate* practice is mentally intentional and energetic. It requires a high level of *intensity* in your focus, repetition, and celebration of incremental successes, which combine to accelerate sustainable change.[22]

As Geoff Colvin, senior editor-at-large for *Fortune* magazine writes, "[Deliberate practice is] highly demanding mentally. Deliberate practice

---

[22] (Schwartz, Stapp and Beauregard 2005)

is above all an effort of focus and concentration. That is what makes it 'deliberate.'"[23]

Studies have shown that, although some natural talent is necessary, it is usually far less of a success factor than most people realize. In fact, the most important "talent" may be a talent for deliberate practice.

In a 1993 article in *Psychology Review*, the authors explained, "Individual differences, even among elite performers, are closely related to assessed amounts of deliberate practice. Many [of the] characteristics once believed to reflect innate talent are actually the result of intense [extended] practice.[24] Colvin adds, "The great performers isolate remarkably specific aspects of what they do and focus on just those things until they're improved; then it's on to the next aspect."[25]

It so happens that the basic properties that define deliberate practice are also the mechanisms that drive neuroplasticity:

- Value-driven (the change must have high value)
- Self-awareness (you must be self-observant and vigilant)
- Focus on specific attributes (to develop and improve)
- Repetition is crucial (repetition creates new tradition)
- Frequency accelerates the process (high-density practice)
- Reflection and feedback (recognize your progress)
- Celebration (give yourself a rush of neuropeptides that strengthen the learning)

You already have the innate, raw talent necessary to apply these principles to improve your performance. In fact, you may have applied deliberate practice in the past as a way of mastering a skill of some kind. Typically, we use deliberate practice to improve our skills in *physical* tasks and activities. However, it can also help improve *mental* tasks and activities.

---

[23] (Colvin 2008)
[24] (Ericsson, Krampe and Tesch-Romer 1993)
[25] (Colvin 2008)

As you will learn in the coming chapters, by integrating neuroplasticity, synaptic pruning, and deliberate practice with formal axiology (value science) we create a powerful new technology ("Axiogenics") for improving how people *think*.

"*Axiogenic practices*" are techniques that improve and accelerate people's capacity to think valuegenically, to answer The Central Question accurately, and to bring greater value to their lives, families, organizations and communities.

The first axiogenic practice we recommend, and one you can start right now, is to make it a deliberate practice to ask yourself The Central Question as often throughout the day as you can. Ask it before a meeting, when you're interacting with others, when you're writing an email, when you have a decision to make about what action to take—whenever you want to be your best and maximize net value.

In the next chapter, we will begin our exploration of *axiology*: the value science behind mastering the skill of *answering* The Central Question.

• • •

"Watch your thoughts, for they become words.
Watch your words, for they become actions.
Watch your actions, for they become habits.
Watch your habits, for they become character.
Watch your character, for it becomes your destiny."

~ Anonymous

CHAPTER 4

Axiology -
Philosophy and Science

"All sciences are now under the obligation to prepare the ground for the future task of the philosopher, which is to solve the problem of value, to determine the true Hierarchy of Values."

~ *Friedrich Nietzsche*

Introduction

Axiology is the science and study of that which governs the most essential part of our "being."

Science is defined as:

"a branch of knowledge or study dealing with a body of facts or truths systematically arranged and showing the operation of general laws: the mathematical sciences." [26]

Science is the process of determining how things *actually* work *regardless* of how we *think* they should work. Despite what I believe, if I were to jump unaided off a ten-story building there is only one direction I would go. It's a law of nature. Laws of nature are inviolate—you can't break them—you can only work with them or suffer the consequences.

It's irrelevant whether we view these laws as natural phenomena or as the creation of a divine being. When, for all practical purposes, a law has been scientifically validated, it behooves us to view the law as being as immutable and unchangeable as gravity or mathematics.

Axiology is the science and study of the laws that govern the most essential part of our *subjective* "being"—our capacity to conceive and perceive value in ourselves, other people, and in the world. At first glance, this may seem strange and illogical: how can something so subjective be explained or understood scientifically? This is precisely why axiology is such an important, paradigm-shifting science. That's what it does.

• • •

"My own brain is to me the most unaccountable of machinery - always buzzing, humming, soaring roaring diving, and then buried in mud. And why? What's this passion for?"

~ *Virginia Woolf*

---

[26] http://dictionary.reference.com/browse/science (09/26/09)

The Philosophy of Axiology

Like many modern sciences, Axiology has its roots in ancient philosophy.

Axiology (value science) has existed as a *philosophy* for about 2500 years: since the time of Plato and Socrates. It was not until the mid-1900s that it evolved into a formal science (more about that later).

Axiology gets its name from the Greek words, *axia*, meaning 'value' or 'worth,' and *logos*, meaning 'science.' For centuries, numerous philosophers and scientists have studied values and 'goodness.' Among them are John Dewey, Adam Smith, Friedrich Nietzsche, Wilbur Marshall Urban, Rudolf Hermann Lotze, Hugo Münsterberg, E. von Hartmann, G.E. Moore, and Robert S. Hartman.

The Philosophy of Axiology develops theoretical answers to questions regarding value, Values, goodness, morality, and ethics, such as:

- Can 'good' be defined?
- Is there something that all "good" things share?
- Is the value of something objective or subjective?
- Is there a relationship between value and goodness?
- Can 'value' and 'goodness' be objectively identified and measured in any way or are they purely subjective?
- If 'value' and 'goodness' could be measured, how would this change our view of what is "moral" and "ethical"?

There are libraries full of books and papers concerning these philosophical questions. In the next several sections, we will attempt to boil it all down to the essentials that are most relevant to understanding your life, the world you live in, and how value structures and value choices affect both.

You have learned that human beings are meaning/value-making machines: *value drives the mind-brain*. Each of us has a different *personal value hierarchy*: the subjective order in which we perceive the relative value of things in our world. What seems "good, moral and ethical" to one person may be quite different to another.

On a larger scale, what is a culture other than a collective value structure that defines the norms of good, bad, right, and wrong for the people in that culture? Some cultural value structures are rigidly established by their "leaders" and brutally enforced through indoctrination and authoritative control. Others are more organic, reflecting the composite value structures of its people and their traditions.

Throughout history, irreconcilable differences in cultural value structures have often resulted in conflict and even war. These cultures (or at least the leadership of these cultures) have often tried to justify war on "moral grounds."

The goal of axiological *philosophy* is to understand the nature of value in the universe *and* man's relationship to that universe through his value structures. Is there a natural order to value—a universal value structure? If there were, then just like the laws of physics, by understanding these "laws of value," we would have a common understanding upon which to create greater value. This would allow us to become better people and to create better organizations and societies; perhaps even to solve many of the world's problems.

Formal axiological science proves that such a universal structure does exist. Before we elaborate on the science, let's explore the philosophy behind it. Then we'll explore how axiology has been transformed through scientific methodology to become a formal science. Finally, we will reveal how formal axiology has achieved its purpose: finding the *Universal Hierarchy of Value* that transcends subjective morals and ethics and provides a logical, mathematical foundation for both maximizing and optimizing goodness in the world.

It's All About Adding Value!

> "Every art and every inquiry, and similarly every action and
> pursuit, is thought to aim at some good; and for this reason the
> good has rightly been declared to be that at which all things
> aim . . . If, then, there is some end of the things we do, which we
> desire for its own sake (everything else being desired for the sake
> of this), and if we do not choose everything for the sake of
> something else (for at that rate the process would go on to
> infinity, so that our desire would be empty and vain), clearly this
> must be the good and the chief good. Will not the knowledge of
> it, then, have a great influence on life?"
>
> ~ Aristotle, in Nicomachean Ethic

What Aristotle alludes to in the above quotation is that everything in our lives—all of mankind's inventions, actions, ideas, laws, systems and norms, including our ethics and Values—exist for one ultimate purpose: to improve our quality of life.

The famous psychologist, Abraham Maslow, spoke of a "Hierarchy of Needs"—physiological (survival), security (safety), social (a sense of belonging), esteem (a sense of self-worth), and self-actualization (personal growth and fulfillment of one's potential). As we move up Maslow's Hierarchy of Needs, from survival to self-actualization, we can see an increasing focus on *quality* of life.

Axiology is the science of value and how value judgments relate to our ability to increase our quality of life. As you will learn in this chapter, *value* also has a hierarchy—a *Hierarchy of Value*.

It is tempting to enter into a rather lengthy logical, philosophical, and even scientific discussion to prove that all things in the Universe are always working toward goodness. Debates about the fundamental purpose of life, and the view that it is simply to add value, are quite fun and mind-expanding. For our purposes here, however, we are simply going to assume that, at the very least, YOU have a desire to maximize the goodness and value in *your* life, which includes the lives of those around you.

As stated earlier, it is human nature to act in accordance with what we *perceive* as being good, the best, or having the greatest value. Depending on whether we are being self-centric or valuegenic, our perceptions and choices may be quite different. Clearly, our perception is sometimes inaccurate and we may make mistakes or fail to produce the value (do the good) we intended. All too often, we recognize our mistakes only with the clarity and perspective of 20/20 hindsight.

Through our genetic make-up, life experiences, education, and our sometimes-limited perceptions, the value/meaning-making machinery of the human mind begins to formulate a personal "philosophy of life." This is how we develop our personal value hierarchy (value structure), and along with it, our habits of mind, behavior patterns, and the perspectives by which we view things. Our ever-evolving personal value hierarchy becomes both the foundation and the filter of all our choices, actions, and reactions—both good and bad. Moreover, because we then filter new experiences through our personal value hierarchy, what we think things mean and the subsequent perspectives we adopt, even our hindsight may not be 20/20.

What if you could know in advance which choices and actions would create the greatest net value? What if you had a framework by which to improve your capacity to recognize the difference between *potentially* good and bad choices? What if you could better predict the potential net value of each possible choice and action? What if you could have 20/20 *fore*sight? Would it help you answer The Central Question? This is what axiology can provide.

Meet Dr. Hartman

The person credited with developing the *formal science* of axiology, almost single-handedly, is Dr. Robert S. Hartman. Dr. Hartman possessed three doctorate-level degrees: mathematics, philosophy, and law.

Dr. Hartman was born in Germany and became an adult during the period that Adolf Hitler was coming into power. At the time, he was a courtroom judge and under great pressure to support what he viewed as evil atrocities by the Nazi regime. He and his family quickly fled Germany with a deep conviction that if "evil" could be organized, so could goodness. This marked the beginning of his life-long quest to understand the nature and definition of goodness.

> "[My goal] is to lift the social disciplines, the so-called
> humanities, to the level of sciences. Then we could know with
> exactness about goodness and value. The moral, religious,
> political, sociological, and other phenomenon [sic] which are
> vague, badly defined and hence badly understood, could
> become objects of exact science. We could become more aware
> of the importance of the miracles and problems of everyday
> living, the things that really matter—the beauty of God's world,
> the laughter of children, the suffering of men, the importance of
> love and compassion."
>
> ~ Dr. Robert S. Hartman [27]

During his life, he went on to hold professorships at Yale, the Massachusetts Institute of Technology, the National University of Mexico, Ohio State, and The University of Tennessee. He held more than 50 lectureships throughout the world. He authored more than 10 books, translated another six books (he spoke nine languages), and wrote hundreds of articles for professional journals of scientific and philosophical merit. By 1970, Dr. Hartman had given two tremendous gifts to the world: The Universal Hierarchy of Value, and the Hartman Value Profile (HVP). He received a nomination for the 1972 Nobel Peace Prize for his life's work in promoting human self-understanding. He was also a pioneer in applying value science to business economics in the area of profit sharing. This part of his work became the basis of the original 401k retirement savings plan (quite different from what we have today). Sadly, he passed away in 1973 while still working to develop this amazing science.

---

[27] (R. S. Hartman, Freedom to Live: The Robert Hartman Story 1994, 56)

Defining Good

> "I can't tell you what goodness is, I can only tell you what it is like. It is like the sun that radiates everything, that warms everything, that makes everything fertile and brings everything forth."
>
> ~ Socrates

The primary question that defined Dr. Hartman's life's work was "What is 'good' and how is 'goodness' organized?" After decades of research, he was able to arrive at this universal definition:

*A thing is good when it has all the properties (attributes)
it needs to fulfill its purpose (intention).*

For example, for an object to be correctly called a "good chair" it must have at least these four properties: a base, a seat that is about knee-high, a back, and sufficient structure to hold it all together. If any of these attributes are missing, it is not a good chair because it cannot fulfill the purpose of a chair.

Suppose on Planet X, the people are very short, say 12 inches. "Knee-high," then, might mean about three inches. On Planet X, an earth-chair would not serve the purpose of a chair because it is not knee-high to the people on Planet X. To them, our chairs would be "no good."

So, inherent in this definition is the need to be able to *conceive* what properties a thing needs to have to fulfill the purpose of the person it is intended to serve.

A good car for *you* needs to have all the properties of a good car as *you* define or conceive it. However, if both you and your spouse will be using the car, then a good car would be one that has all the properties that both you *and* your spouse think a good car should have.

The *relative* goodness of something is determined by the degree to which it can fulfill its purpose. That is, how many of the required properties it has. Clearly, a thing could have only *some* of the properties.

Generally, the more it matches the properties in its definition, the "better" it is (the greater its goodness) and the more of its purpose it can fulfill. A "bad" thing is something that cannot fulfill its purpose at all because it does not have a sufficient number of the properties necessary to fulfill its purpose.

For example, we might say that a comedian is an excellent comedian when every joke is funny. If 80% of his jokes are funny, he might be considered a very good comedian. At the other end of the spectrum, if none of his jokes are funny, he might be considered a bad comedian.

In this case, whose definition of 'funny' matters? If an audience isn't laughing, is it a bad comedian or a bad audience? Perhaps it's just a matter of one's perspective. The goodness of something may vary depending on the perspective of the person or persons who are defining the purpose and who are determining the properties needed to fulfill it.

If you are providing a service, how important is it to know the customer's definition of "good service" if you are to fulfill your purpose of delivering value to the customer?

If the comedian's purpose is to earn money making other people laugh, then to fulfill his purpose, he has to tell jokes that fulfill the audience's (his customer's) definition of funny. One audience may think self-deprecating sarcasm is funny, while another may think satire is hilarious. However, if the comedian's definition of funny is whatever makes him laugh, *and that's all he cares about*, then anything *he* thinks is funny will do.

If an audience doesn't laugh, a self-centric comedian would say it's a bad audience—"they don't laugh at my jokes." A value-centric comedian would take accountability, by recognizing that his jokes did not meet the definition of 'funny' for that audience.

As you can see, there is a bit more to Dr. Hartman's definition of good than initially meets the eye. Specifically:

- A thing is good when it has all the properties (attributes) it needs to fulfill its purpose (intention).

- There are degrees of goodness (e.g., bad, fair, good, very good, excellent) determined by the degree to which a thing has the properties it needs to fulfill its purpose.
- The "purpose" of something can be defined, and defined differently, by all for whom the thing is intended to serve.

As you learned earlier, we all have our own unique value structure. Your personal value structure is the basis upon which you define what's good, bad, and valuable *to you*. It also affects your ability to perceive and understand how others may define goodness.

Putting all this together, we have an expanded definition of goodness: *A thing has goodness to the degree that it has all the properties (attributes) it needs to fulfill the purpose of the person or persons it is intended to serve.*

"Mark" is a brilliant man. His knowledge, artistic eye, and quick mind allow him to instantly see how to solve almost any problem in his field of expertise: cosmetic surgery. Unfortunately, Dr. Mark had a hard time fulfilling his purpose of helping people feel better about their appearance, and his business was suffering as a result.

The problem? When prospective patients came to his office for a consultation about a perceived "flaw" in their appearance, he would see and point out other "flaws" that he could also fix. He was genuinely interested in helping them and it really wasn't about the money. However, the way he communicated his suggestions made prospective patients feel worse about themselves—even more flawed—and they often interpreted his suggestions as a way for him to make more money. Clearly he was miscommunicating his intentions. Dr. Mark really struggled with it: his heart ached because he felt his intentions were misunderstood and he didn't understand why.

Dr. Mark's real problem was that he failed to understand his prospective patients' intentions. They believed that all they needed to do was get the one "flaw" in their self-image "fixed" and they would feel better about themselves, be more attractive, and more confident. Inadvertently, he was robbing them of their hope by pointing out "flaws" they hadn't seen. Despite his good intentions, too often he failed to convert prospective patients into actual patients. This prevented him from being able to fulfill either his or his prospective patients' purposes. His business was "no good" and he was starting to think that *he* was "no good."

Once Mark understood the concept of purpose, the definition of goodness, and a few other axiogenic principles, he completely turned around his business and his life. He was then able to discern his patients' intentions and communicate with them in a way that gave them the hope they needed.

Good for Us

Is it ever possible for something to fulfill differing intentions (purposes) and still have the exact same set of properties? Absolutely! If your intention for putting up a bird feeder is to give the birds food and my purpose is to attract birds to my window so I can watch them, then putting up a bird feeder close to the window fulfills both our intentions.

Note: From this point onward, we will use the words "intention, purpose, meaning, and definition" somewhat synonymously. You could say, we suppose, that we will use whichever word seems to best fulfill our purpose!

When we experience conflict, it is usually because of a difference in perception regarding *properties*, rather than intentions, even though people often seem to be arguing over intentions.

Jim and Phoebe, business partners, were arguing over which marketing strategy would be the best use of their company's limited marketing budget. Jim wanted to pursue an advertising campaign. Phoebe wanted to spend the money on a public relations campaign. Jim argued that the media advertising had a more measurable and direct return on investment. Phoebe believed that public relations would ultimately bring in more revenues.

As far as Jim was concerned, the intention was to generate quick, direct, measurable results. Phoebe felt the intention was to establish more credibility and affinity in the marketplace. Jim couldn't see how public relations could fulfill his intention and Phoebe couldn't see how advertising could fulfill her intention. Clearly, there was a gap between what each perceived as the purpose of their marketing initiative.

During a joint coaching call, Jim and Phoebe discovered common ground on a more fundamental level: the mutual intention to bring in new business. I then asked them to take a valuegenic approach and set aside their own ideas so they could explore the merit of each other's ideas and intentions. This allowed a healthier discussion regarding the properties and attributes of various options, which resulted in a gain-gain solution that they were both very excited about.

Months later, they reported that business was booming. The solution they created together was generating higher revenues than either had projected their own solution would produce.

Maximum value in any partnership (business or personal) is created when win-win solutions are found. Even better are what we call *gain-gain* solutions. An ideal gain-gain solution is one that has the properties needed to fulfill both your intention and your partner's intention without taking value away from either. To have a workable partnership, you don't have to agree on the intention; you just need to create solutions that fulfill, as much as possible, *both* of your intentions. This is the essence of valuegenic compromise and co-creativity, and it sheds light on the importance of understanding other people's purposes, intentions, and desires if you want to optimize value generation.

Defining Value

Thus far, we have defined "good," but we have not defined "value." Just because two things equally fulfill their purpose, does not mean that they are of equal value. If there is an objective definition of "good," is there also an objective definition of "value"? Yes, there is, but before we get to it, it's important to lay a bit more foundation.

We could probably all objectively agree that a good house has more *value* than a good pencil. That's easy. However, not all valuations are quite so simple or obvious. How about comparing a bird feeder and a bird, or a factory and a government; which of these has greater value? Some people would say the bird feeder; others the bird. Some would say a government has more value than a factory. Is there a "right" answer? Is there an objective way to resolve subjective differences? Yes.

Dr. Hartman believed, and ultimately proved, that value is objectively measurable. That is, all things have a natural, objective value independent of the valuer's subjective perception. (Note: the "value" we are discussing is *relative* value: the value of one thing in comparison to the value of another.)

Dr. Hartman wrote, "The difference between natural science and value science is that the former applies to events [and things], while the latter applies to *the meaning* of events [and things]. Value, we may say, is *meaning*. When we say that life has meaning, we mean that it has value. The richer its meaning, the richer its value. When we say that life has no meaning, we mean that it has no value. The poorer its meaning, the poorer its value. A meaningless life is without value, is no good."[28]

---

[28] (R. S. Hartman, Freedom to Live: The Robert Hartman Story 1994, 88)

In other words, a thing has value to the degree that it has meaning. In human terms, to have meaning is to have purpose. Then what is the objective yardstick for meaning or purpose?

The answer is amazingly simple. Let's go back to Dr. Hartman's definition of "good": a thing is good when it has all the properties (attributes) it needs to fulfill its purpose (intention). Consider that each individual property, in and of itself, has meaning and purpose in regards to the greater definition or intention of the whole. One property cannot be replaced by a different property if the thing is to fulfill its intention. For example, you can't substitute a car engine with a hamster and still have it be a good car.

If every property has meaning and purpose (and therefore, value), then it follows that *the greater the number of properties a thing has to have in order to fulfill its purpose, the greater its value.*

The *potential* for something to acquire or receive needed properties also enhances its value. For example, a broken-down car that can be fixed cost-effectively has more value than one that cannot. A person who is seen as having the *potential* to be a great friend, spouse, singer, or athlete, is often valued (by the valuer) more than those who are perceived as not having such potential.

By the objective definition of value, a bicycle has less value than a motorcycle, which has less value than a car, because each has progressively more properties. Likewise, a bird has greater value than a bird feeder because life has many more properties (potential) than inanimate (non-living) objects.

To take it one step further, how about comparing the flavors of strawberry and chocolate? Is there an objective value difference? Probably not; they both have the same basic purpose (to give flavor) and may even have the same number of objective properties. However, if your eight-year-old daughter wants a chocolate birthday cake, it's better to buy her a chocolate cake rather than a strawberry one because only the chocolate cake has the property of "she likes it."

To summarize:

- **A thing is *good* when it has all the properties (attributes) it needs to fulfill its purpose (intention).**
  Example: A chair that has a base, a back, is knee-high, and is stable enough to hold a person.

- **The greater the number of properties a thing must have to fulfill its purpose, the greater its value.**
  Example: A space shuttle has greater value than a bicycle. (Based on properties, not financial value; although, in the world, things with a higher number of properties tend to be given a higher price.)

- **A thing has *goodness* to the degree that it has all the properties (attributes) it needs to fulfill the purpose of the person or persons it is intended to serve.**
  Example: A baker is a good baker to the degree that he bakes delicious baked goods that his customers want and enjoy.

- **The relative value of things is objective in nature and subjective in our perceptions.**
  Example: Doing the right thing has greater objective value than being right (getting your way). However, subjectively, not everyone sees it that way.

What does all this add up to in practical application? If the actual value of something is X, but you perceive it as Z, you will have made a subjective error in your value judgment. There will be a gap between your value perception and the actual value and it will likely cost you something. Likewise, if you think the value of something is A and I think it's C, then there is a gap between your perception and mine. That gap could easily cost one or both of us if we can't reconcile it.

So long as any such unreconciled gaps exist value cannot be optimize, let alone maximized. Through proper practice, people can improve their perceptive abilities. When they do, they become better at recognizing and reconciling gaps and, thus, achieve greater success.

What is 'Moral' Goodness?

Dr. Hartman's definition of good is objectively universal. However, the *application* of the definition is subjective in that each person may have a different *concept* of something's definition or purpose, as well as a different *perception* of whether or not it has the properties it needs.

Dr. Hartman's definition refers to the *objective* goodness of things, not their *moral* goodness. Based on his definition, can there be such a thing as a good thief, a good murderer, or a good tyrant? Yes, as long as they have all the attributes needed to fulfill the definition of a thief, murderer, or tyrant.

> Are you thinking, "How can something as bad as a murderer be good? What about terrorists, cancer, earthquakes, starvation, and my ex-spouse—how can these be any good? They certainly exist, but I see no good in them whatsoever!"
>
> Take a breath. Remember, we're not saying any of these are *morally* good or that their intention/purpose is good. So far, we've only looked at goodness as an ability to fulfill an intention, definition, meaning, or purpose.

So, now let's look at how we can define *moral goodness*. The battle over what constitutes "moral right and good" has been raging for thousands of years and is a primary source of conflict in politics, between religions, and between cultures. To resolve these conflicts, it is important that we learn to distinguish moral goodness from objective goodness, and find some common ground on a definition of "moral."

We established earlier that goodness is a function of having the properties necessary to fulfill an intention or purpose. According to the dictionary, the definition of 'moral' is: "(adj.) of or concerned with the judgment of goodness or badness of human action and character . . .

arising from conscience or the sense of right and wrong."[29] So, 'moral' goodness adds the concept of *right and wrong.*

Combining our definition of 'good' with this definition of 'moral,' we can say that someone or something is morally good or right when it supports the creation of greater net value *in reality*, and morally bad or wrong when it diminishes or destroys net value *in reality.*

Murder and thievery are morally wrong ("evil") because they take away net value. Love is morally good because it adds value. Dr. Mark was not morally evil in his failure to fulfill his intentions, he was just not very good at *fulfilling* his intentions; he was missing important properties, namely, an understanding of his patients' intentions.

Notice that in the dictionary definition of 'moral,' it says, "the *judgment* of goodness or badness of human action and character… arising from *conscience.*" Clearly, 'moral goodness' is a matter of judgment (subjective) and requires a conscience to help us recognize and define what is *morally* good and to act in morally good ways—to add value.

Only people can be morally good or morally evil. A knife can be a good knife (it is sharp) or a bad knife (it is dull), but in and of itself, it is neither morally good nor evil. While it has the potential to be an *instrument* of good (cooking) or evil (killing), only the *person using* the knife (e.g., surgeon, murderer) and the *act* of that person (e.g., surgery, murder) can be morally good or evil.

> Isn't it interesting that to "live" a good and moral life is to add value to life, whereas an "evil" life is one that takes away value? Notice that "live" spelled backwards is "evil."

Whether we perceive something as being morally good or morally evil will have a lot to do with our own *subjective moral perspective.* Differences in perspective and perception are the primary reasons why so much conflict, stress, distrust, and ill-will exists in the world. Your

---

[29] The American Heritage Dictionary, New College Edition, 1978

definition of what is morally "good" or "right" may be very different from mine. We may each have a different perspective on things, and therefore, perceive things differently.

This all gives rise to some very big questions. Is there an objective approach to making value decisions that can help us resolve subjective differences in the way we perceive things? How can we know for sure what adds or subtracts net value, who's "right," and who's "wrong"? Can we objectively measure and determine the value of one thing compared to another? Ultimately, how do we optimize value *in reality*?

What you are about to learn is how *formal* (scientific) axiology reveals the *Universal Hierarchy of Value*—the natural order or "structure" of value in the universe. Furthermore, through formal axiology we can *objectively* measure how well your personal value structure aligns with the natural order. Then, by integrating that information with the principles of neuroplasticity and deliberate practice, you can learn to intentionally change and improve how you operate in the world. You can dramatically improve your natural ability to ask, answer, and act on The Central Question, thus, maximizing your success!

· · ·

The Formal Science of Axiology is Born

> The science of formal axiology may be one of the most important developments in human history.

How fortuitous for us that Dr. Hartman had three such diverse doctorate-level degrees (philosophy, mathematics, and law). The combination gave him a unique perspective from which to explore the scientific nature of goodness and value. Dr. Hartman applied mathematics to the philosophy of axiology, just as Sir Isaac Newton applied mathematics to the philosophy of physics. Through mathematics, Newton discovered the *Law of Universal Gravitation*. Likewise, through mathematics, Dr. Hartman discovered what's called the *Universal Hierarchy of Value*. The

Hierarchy of Value provides the universal framework for what objectively *IS* of greater and lesser value.

We can easily see a parallel between Newton's and Hartman's work. While Newton's gravity is based on an object's mass, Dr. Hartman's axiological hierarchy is based on the properties of things. The greater mass something has the greater its gravity (or gravity's pull on the thing; its weight), while the greater number of properties something has the greater its value (and its "pull" on us). Isn't it interesting how we sometimes use the words "weight" and "gravity" when we are describing something of great value or importance?

How important is Dr. Hartman's discovery of the Hierarchy of Value? Given our understanding that value drives many of the processes of our "inner" world, Dr. Hartman's discovery is every bit as important as the discoveries of the scientists and mathematicians that have helped us to understand and master the "physical" world.

What enabled this discovery is Dr. Hartman's realization that just as we perceive the physical world in multiple dimensions, we also make value judgments in multiple dimensions.

"Though the measure of value [through formal axiology] is universal and objective, it should be noted that the application is subjective."[30]

~ Dr. Robert S. Hartman

• • •

The Primary Dimensions of Value

People first, productivity second, policy third.

What follows is an explanation of each of the primary dimensions of value. Together they form the framework of axiology and the basis for the "value" in "Axiogenics."

---

[30] (R. S. Hartman, Freedom to Live: The Robert Hartman Story 1994, 89)

> Imprint this framework on your heart and in your mind. You and your world will be better for it.

The Systemic Dimension

A *systemic* valuation looks at a system and determines its value dualistically. A thing must have *all* of the properties needed to fulfill its purpose, or it doesn't fulfill its purpose at all. Systemically, a thing is all or nothing, black or white, right or wrong, perfect or non-existent; there is no in-between.

Like an idea, for example; either an idea exists or it does not exist. Can you think of an idea that does not exist? At the very moment you think of one, it exists. Ideas are the building blocks of mental constructs. When you say, "I have no idea," it means you have no mental construct for that which you have no idea about. Therefore, mental constructs are systemic. Examples of mental constructs (man/mind-made systems) include: laws, logic, theories, ideals, dreams, goals, expectations, rituals, procedures, rules, strategies, aspirations, engineering, and grammar. Thinking, itself, is systemic. Nature also provides examples of systemic things: ecosystems, weather systems, photosynthesis, nervous systems, etc. Either a proton, for example, exists or it doesn't exist. These all are systems or norms upon which or within which we operate.

A systemic thing exists only as part of a larger system. For example, you have a nervous system, a circulatory system, a respiratory system, an endocrine system, a thinking system, and a digestive system. All of these are part of a system called the human body. Your human body is part of a social system, a cultural set of norms and traditions operating under the rule of local law with communication systems, economic systems and political systems. These systems operate with the global systems of economics and politics. All nations and cultures must also function within the systems of nature, such as bio-systems and eco-systems. Our planet exists as part of a solar system, which, in turn, is just one part in the larger system of the universe.

When we assess the systemic value of something, we are assessing its capacity to add value (fulfill its purpose) within the larger concept of which the thing is or could be a part. Does it play its part in the system by making it work or does it keep the system from working?

A systemic valuation does not distinguish between the concept of reality and the perception of reality: systemically, perception *is* reality.

For example, an expectation is a systemic mental construct, ideal or visual mental image of how something should be or is going to be (concept). If we perceive that something isn't the way it's "supposed" to be, it's "wrong." If it is the way it's supposed to be, it's "right." If some*one* isn't the way we expect them to be, we say they are "wrong." Our perception, that something or someone is either right or wrong, then becomes our "reality." To us they *are* right or they *are* wrong, they can't be both. Yet *that* reality only exists in our systemic imagination, our "mind's eye." Nature's reality has no right or wrong, only what is. Only human nature judges right and wrong.

These systemic judgments can easily result in inappropriate (inaccurate) valuations of people, ideas, processes, and things. When someone agrees with our idea, or we think they see things the same way we see them, we may inadvertently jump to the all or nothing conclusion that they will agree with us on everything.

An error in systemic valuation is an error in judging how things (including people) will, are, ought to, or could be. These misjudgments can confuse our perception and, therefore, undermine our understanding of what it might take to make things better or to achieve a goal. If you've made erroneous assumptions, and you don't have a complete and accurate picture of knowing where you are, it's difficult to know what to do to get to where you want to be.

Systemically, we can become very attached to our own ideas and perceptions because we so strongly believe we are "right" and we certainly don't like being "wrong." Therefore, we may have a hard time seeing things from any perspective other than our own.

How often have you taken a systemic (black and white) perspective and allowed it to get in the way of a healthy relationship? When you refuse to consider another perspective because, from your perspective, you already "know" you are "right," you are making a systemic judgment. There is always more than one perspective from which to look at things, but when a systemic thought process gets locked-in, it can be very hard to see any other perspective.

Just as you may be attached to *your* "right" idea, so might others be attached to *their* "right" idea. When we approach a disagreement in a purely systemic way, we're forced to make a choice between making them "wrong" or letting them be "right" even when we think they're wrong. Can you see how this can cause problems?

Most ideas for solving problems have multiple parts to them. Each part has a value of its own pertaining to how the idea may contribute to the fulfillment of a larger purpose (solving the problem). What often happens, however, is that we judge the whole idea systemically, and if we perceive any one part of the idea as bad or wrong, we may dismiss (dis-value) the whole idea. Moreover, the *person* who had the idea may be left feeling *personally* and *wholly* dismissed (disvalued). Since people don't like being disvalued, if this happens too often, the "idea person" is eventually going to stop offering ideas altogether, even their really good ideas.

A better approach is to acknowledge the good parts of an idea, even if you don't agree with the entire idea. In so doing, you don't inadvertently disvalue the person *and* you foster collaboration and co-creativity.

When we have an expectation about what someone was supposed to do, or how something is supposed to be, and reality doesn't seem to conform to our expectations, it causes a gap. This gap or conflict is between two mental constructs: what we had expected to happen and what we perceive did happen.

The brain interprets these unreconciled gaps—conflicting ideas—as "errors" or threats. As a result, we can become uncomfortable, frustrated, upset, or possibly even angry enough to lash out against those who we see as the source of our discomfort and even against those who have nothing to do with the situation.

If we perceive that we, ourselves, are not living up to our own or others' expectations, we may even disvalue ourselves. We may develop limiting beliefs (e.g., "I can never fulfill my intention."), become driven by a need for perfection (e.g., "I MUST fulfill my intention."), or both.

People sometimes believe that "good intentions" are enough. Therefore, if their intentions are not fulfilled it must be something or someone else's fault (since "good intentions" can't be wrong). This can lead to a lack of accountability ("It's not my fault."), blaming other people or other things ("It's the hammer's fault I banged my finger."), feelings of obligation ("The world is making me do this."), and a host of other stress-inducers; quickly throwing "life" out of balance.

The words 'should', 'must', 'need', 'have to', 'always', and 'never' are systemic and are often indicative of unbalanced systemic thinking. Remember the amygdala hijack? It's usually systemically-driven. Something happens that doesn't conform to our expectations or intentions about how things should be (a gap) and it becomes a threat. Since perception and reality are, to the systemic mind, one and the same, the perceived threat looks like an actual threat and we instantly react.

During an amygdala hijack, we most often react in ways that disvalue others. We can emotionally crush people in the name of "right and wrong." Sometimes we don't realize we're doing it until it's too late.

If your desire is to learn how to create greater value in your life, it is important to realize that the systemic dimension is of the least value of the three primary dimensions because it has the least number of valuational properties—two. Yet, for many people, it is this dimension that most dominates their thinking, actions, and reactions. The systemic dimension is running your life to the degree that you:

- have right/wrong battles with other people
- see things as pass or fail, win or lose, all or nothing
- get upset when something doesn't go "your way"

- defend and justify your ideas and opinions to the point of detriment or frustration for yourself and others
- spend time dreaming/fantasizing about what your life could be like if only something were different
- have perfectionist tendencies
- resist doing anything that isn't "your way"
- feel that you have no control or must have control
- have a need to conform or to not conform at any price
- have feelings of obligation or duty
- expect instant gratification
- focus on outcomes rather than processes

Does it sound like the systemic dimension itself is a "bad" thing? In truth, the systemic dimension has significant goodness and value when used appropriately. A full and accurate value judgment cannot exclude systemic valuation because everything has some level of systemic value. Even an out-of-balance systemic tendency can support success in some areas of life. For example, dreams, goals, and possibilities are powerful motivators ("I can see it so clearly I can almost touch it."). As social beings, it's important to distinguish between right and wrong, good and bad.

To get things done efficiently and effectively, understanding and creating systems and systematic methodologies is very useful. If you think about it, every process or system broken down to its smallest granularity is really a collection or string of systemic events and conditions. Being able to see the parts of things at this level of detail can be extremely helpful in pinpointing errors or breakdowns in the system, rather than simply throwing out the whole system.

Here's an example: you get in your car and turn the key; nothing happens. Would you react by saying "This car is no good," or would you more rationally conclude that the battery or some other part (property) of the car is no good (malfunctioning)?

If we can conceptually separate a system (e.g., a car) into its smaller parts or sub-systems, we can make better, more precise, systemic valuations. Rather than scrapping the whole car, for example, we can look for the one part that isn't working to support the system. Then we know which part needs fixing to make the whole system work again. This same principle applies to any and every system: from cars to computers, from digestive systems to healthcare systems, and from educational systems to political systems.

We express value-centeredness in the systemic dimension as the desire to do the right thing because it *adds the most value to the larger system,* not just because it is "right." The systemic mind is a primary source of motivation, creativity, and vision for a greater possibility. Having a high capacity to think systemically allows the mind to make clear connections (mentally "connecting the dots") between a string of dualistic causes and effects. This helps us solve problems, improve systems, invent new things, and produce better results.

Systemically, answering The Central Question—*What choice can I make and action can I take, in this moment, to create the greatest net value?*—usually requires that we:

- let go of any strong attachments to our own ideas, "shoulds," and "oughts,"
- embrace what is (the actual existing conditions),
- listen to other ideas and perspectives,
- explore new and different possibilities,
- work to "connect the dots," and
- avoid making things personal or taking things personally.

A person with a high capacity in the systemic dimension sees both the whole *and* the parts as a system of systems. They are able to perceive the real value in conformity, in teamwork, and in establishing and obeying laws, policies, and procedures. Their own ideas and agendas will *contribute* to the greater net value rather than *compete* with it. Such a person isn't concerned with whose idea something is. Their only concern is the whether or not the idea can add value.

What would happen if, instead of allowing our systemic, black-and-white mind to take over and create an amygdala hijack, we chose a different perspective—one that sees "shades and colors," a greater richness of properties than just two (dualistic)? How would this impact our choices and reactions? Would it keep us from going on "tilt"? Would it help us make better choices, to be more understanding, to collaborate more, or to see things we could not see before? Would it help us create greater value because we can perceive greater value? Absolutely!

This brings us to the extrinsic dimension—the next highest level of value and valuing, where both intention and the properties are more complex and relative than absolute and black and white.

The Extrinsic Dimension

The *extrinsic* dimension deals with things defined and valued by substance and function, usually in relationship or comparison to some other thing external to itself. This is the dimension in which our five senses operate. What we can hear, see, taste, touch, and smell are the extrinsic properties of things (though the meaning or value that we give to what we sense may not always be extrinsic). Extrinsic things can be both tangible, such as a chair, and intangible, such as time. Because extrinsic things are measurable, we judge things in the extrinsic dimension as having more or less value relative to other things in the extrinsic dimension (e.g. more or less, bigger or smaller, longer or shorter, etc.).

Extrinsic things have a finite (countable and limited) number of properties. The number of properties can be huge, nearly infinite, but never quite reaching true infinity (mathematicians call it "denumerably infinite"). Furthermore, things valued extrinsically are not unique. Any two or more items with essentially the same set of properties can be substituted one for the other. In a basic sense, one chair is just as good as any other chair of the same design and quality.

Keeping in mind that the number of properties in the extrinsic dimension can approach infinity, we see that virtually everything tangible, from a rock to a space shuttle, is extrinsic in nature. In the extrinsic dimension, we begin to see degrees of goodness or quality. For example, a chair with a slightly wobbly leg is still a chair, but perhaps not as good a chair as one with four sturdy legs. Unlike the systemic dimension, in which something either is or isn't (to be or not to be), in the extrinsic dimension things can be "more" or "less."

The extrinsic value of something (including a person or an idea) is expressed in terms of how it increases our capacity to add value (quality) to life—to get things done, to make money, to feel good, to reach a goal—efficiently and effectively. If not for human beings, money, for example, would have no value or purpose; nor would trains, planes, computers, rocking chairs, or cell phones. Ideas, rules, laws, and social systems wouldn't exist. Obviously, the purpose of man-made things, both tangible and intangible, is to serve man's intentions.

When a person is lacking (or slacking) in the ability to *conceive* what properties and attributes a thing needs (or doesn't need) to fulfill its purpose, they will not have a viable standard by which to make value judgments. Consequently, they may not be able to make good value judgments. When a person is lacking in the capacity to *perceive* whether or not a thing *has* the properties it needs, they are also less likely to make good value choices.

For example, if you don't know what properties a good car needs to have, it may be difficult to know whether or not a specific car is a good one. Similarly, even if you know what a good car is, if you don't have the means to know whether or not a specific car has the necessary properties, it's difficult to know if it's a good car or not.

As previously stated, we can substitute one extrinsic thing for another similar extrinsic thing. For example, you can use any number of modes of transportation to get from one place to another. A big blue car will get you to where you want to go just as well as a little green car.

One is only better than another based on the traveler's preferences or intentions: fast, inexpensive, relaxing, safe, etc.

In the extrinsic dimension, everything is relative. To determine the value of one option over another, we compare the required cost (time, effort, resources), and projected benefits (value) of each option. One person may value money or time more than another person values them and, therefore, make different choices. Usually, an expendable resource used on one project or task is a resource that cannot be used for any other project or task. For this reason, we set priorities and allocate resources where we think they will produce the greatest value.

Money is extrinsic. It has a purpose outside of itself. How many people overvalue money so much that acquiring it at almost any cost becomes a major driving force in their life? A person may so value getting "rich," for example, that he may undervalue his family, his integrity, and even his own health in the pursuit of making money. Of course, there are also those who don't value saving money enough and, as a consequence, run into trouble when unexpected expenses arise.

Time is also extrinsic in that it is a resource. How many people do you know who have trouble "managing time"? How often do people say, "But, I don't have time"? Notice how quickly our thoughts about time can become systemic. What's actually happening is that their value structures and priorities are in conflict, misaligned, or unclear to them. As a result, they struggle to find a way to fulfill all their intentions. How often have you felt that people didn't have time for you or you didn't have time for someone else? When people overvalue "their" time, how much less cooperative and helpful are they likely to be when someone asks for help?

Can you see how conflicting agendas, intentions, and valuations easily create conflict over the use of extrinsic resources (e.g., time and money)? What would happen if we communicated our intentions and cared to listen to the intentions of others more often? Would we see and experience less stress and conflict?

Extrinsic valuations help us to see how actions, methods, tools, knowledge, talent, and resources can help us add value in the most efficient and effective manner. Therefore, our capacity to make good extrinsic valuations will determine how well we utilize our time, energy, and resources to improve quality of life.

When we fail to make accurate extrinsic valuations, we are likely to make errors in judgment about what needs doing, how best to go about doing it, and how to best allocate our resources. We can misread the magnitude of problems and obstacles. We may over or undervalue material things, possessions, and even the value of the results our actions produce. As a result, we may lack or even have an overabundance of focus, energy, passion, enthusiasm, order, or structure.

Extrinsic misjudgments are often the cause of our failures to take the appropriate actions necessary to fulfill the intentions we have for our lives and the lives of others.

We express value-centeredness in the extrinsic dimension by having a commitment to optimize the use of resources (time, money, energy, materials, talents, etc.) so that waste is minimized and net value is maximized. Extrinsically, The Central Question—*What choice can I make and action can I take in this moment to create the greatest net value?*— refers to judgments about the wise use of resources, how best to go about doing things, and the value of *things*.

While the systemic dimension deals with things dualistically (black and white), the extrinsic dimension deals with things in relative, comparable terms: most, more, same, less, least; or best, better, good, worse, bad, worst, etc. It is the dimension of *doing*, functionality, practicality, and the allocation of resources.

But, so what? Why is it important to do good things, to do them well, and to make good use of resources? Clearly, there is more to life than just following rules and getting things done, isn't there? Ultimately, the value of everything systemic and everything extrinsic is in their ability to add greater quality to life. Yet "quality of life" can mean very different things to different people. People have different priorities, preferences, goals, jobs, agendas, aspirations, and perceptions. They also may have different talents, experiences, or knowledge. This gives each person a unique set of perspectives on life and a unique set of perceptive abilities.

Every person is unique and irreplaceable. No one can replace my wife. My wife, Pam, did not *replace* my late wife, Margaret; Pam is a different woman with a special and glorious uniqueness all her own, and no one can replace her either.

This brings us to the intrinsic value dimension.

The Intrinsic Dimension

> "The intrinsic value in human beings is their potential to make themselves better people, to make themselves more than they are."
>
> ~ *Captain Jean Luc Picard, from "Star Trek Generations"*

Intrinsic "things" are unique, incomparable, and irreplaceable. An intrinsic thing has infinite value, even when it is lacking some of its extrinsic and systemic properties. Its value is innate unto itself. It defines itself and judges its own value. The intrinsic dimension is the dimension of *being*.

People are the quintessential example of an intrinsic "thing." The axiological definition of value states that the greater the number of properties that something needs to fulfill its intention, the greater its value. That means that anything with (or the potential for) an infinite number of properties must be of infinite value.

Human beings, because they have unique, incomparable, and irreplaceable properties, are of *infinite intrinsic* value. In other words, scientifically, people have *infinitely* greater intrinsic value than all else extrinsic and systemic. It's not just a moral or ethical ideal; it is a scientific fact. Whatever value judgment you make, if you value anything more than the intrinsic value of a human being, you are violating this principle and, ultimately, you will pay a price for it.

Note that we are not talking about the physical body of a person (organs and tissue), but the "life and spirit" of the human being—the conscious self, the "I"—and all the infinite potential that it represents.

Consider this: if you remove a leg from a human being, does this diminish their intrinsic value *as a human being* in any way? Is the life of a one-legged person of any more or less value than a two-legged person?

Throughout history, humankind has intrinsically disvalued others based upon extrinsic properties (physical attributes such as skin color, height, and build) and systemic properties (such as religion, social class, or nationality). Examples abound of people with certain attributes being killed, enslaved, segregated, vilified, or oppressed by people who have different extrinsic and/or systemic attributes. This often leads to a belief that those who look or think differently have more or less intrinsic value. For example: good-looking people are better; educated people are worth more; and short people are inferior.

Believing something does not make it true. How many of our beliefs, at some point in life, turn out to be false? Axiologically, regardless of whatever extrinsic or systemic attributes someone has, every human being has equal intrinsic value—*infinite* value!

Consider all the good that people with physical challenges have created in the world: Steven Hawking, Helen Keller, and Beethoven (who wrote many of his masterpieces *after* he became deaf) are just a few. Indeed, who among us does not have some level of physical, mental, or emotional "shortcoming"? Yet also, who among us does not have an infinite array of possibilities and potentials in our lives?

Again, all human beings are of infinite value. By this logic, we must acknowledge that Adolf Hitler and Jack the Ripper are of equal *intrinsic* value to a priest or the President. Each has infinite intrinsic value as a human being, no more or less than any other person. However, that does not make their character or their actions *morally* equal, and it certainly does not mean they have the same extrinsic or systemic value.

Say What?

How can a murderer be of equal value to a priest? Both the priest and the murderer are human beings. Both fulfill the definition of the intrinsic human being. Therefore, they are of equal value *intrinsically*. However, based on our value judgments in other dimensions (systemic and extrinsic), we treat them differently. For example, we judge murder to be wrong and we value protecting people from murders. Therefore, we put murders in jail when we catch them.

The intrinsic dimension is the realm of *being*. It encompasses all the immeasurable, intangible *qualities* of life: love, compassion, empathy, intuition, sadness, grief, joy, security, wholeness, faith, trust, etc.

Because the intrinsic dimension is infinite, one cannot overvalue it. Intrinsic valuation is a measure of uniqueness. When assessing the value of something from an intrinsic perspective, we are measuring its unique ability and/or potential to fulfill a unique purpose. To undervalue the intrinsic *requires* that we overvalue something extrinsic or systemic. Remember, nothing is worth more than the intrinsic. This is why *nothing is more important than the intrinsic value of people first, including you*!

When we fail to appreciate our own intrinsic value, we may see ourselves as being less valuable than someone who we see as more talented, prettier, or smarter (all extrinsic). We may take less care of ourselves because we see it as selfish/wrong (systemic) or even a waste of time to do so (extrinsic).

Whenever we undervalue the unique and intrinsic value of ourselves or other people, we plant the seeds of hate, anger, jealously, and prejudice; easily throwing us into win-lose, me versus you, us versus them mentalities. If we allow these seeds to germinate and grow, it will invariably lead to a loss of productivity, cooperation, performance, joy, happiness, creativity, and more. Failing to acknowledge the infinite value of people is the fundamental cause of virtually all of the world's ills and wars, including the wars waged in the name of idealism or religion. When we undervalue the intrinsic, we run the risk of moral confusion.

How ironic that we can see how, from an axiological perspective, even Adolf Hitler had infinite intrinsic value. Yet Hitler, himself, demonstrated what happens when a charismatic leader fails to recognize the infinite intrinsic value of all people and manages to alter the moral beliefs of an entire population.

Besides people, does anything else have intrinsic value? Remember that the intrinsic dimension of value deals with the unique, irreplaceable, inseparable, and infinite value; including the *qualities* of life. Therefore, things can have intrinsic value *to us* if we see them as unique, irreplaceable, and significant to the quality of our life. Your pet dog or cat, for example, or a family heirloom, may have intrinsic value to you, but probably not to someone else. However, because both the pet and the heirloom are extrinsic by nature (with limits to their potential) they can never truly rise to the infinite value of a human life. With that being said, we all know of people who seem to value their pets or other extrinsic and systemic things more than they value other people.

Now consider The Central Question—*What choice can I make and action can I take in this moment to create the greatest net value?*—from an intrinsic perspective. To a valuegenic person, people come before all else, extrinsic and systemic. They recognize the unique, infinite value of self *and* others and will seek to understand the impact of their choices and actions on themselves *and* other people. They consider other people's concerns, needs, perspectives, opinions, desires, beliefs, and feelings *as well as* their own. Valuegenic people are not *only* concerned with what adds value to them (self-centric), they are concerned with creating greater net value—period—and that includes them.

• • •

The Dimensional Hierarchy

> Conform to the hierarchy and you will always add net value.
> Attempt to violate the hierarchy and you will always limit value.

Technically, we can express each value dimension (systemic, extrinsic, and intrinsic) in terms of transfinite mathematics. However, explaining the complex mathematics is beyond the intention of this book. So let's keep it simple and logical.

The more properties a thing needs to have to fulfill its intention (to be good), the higher its value. Since the intrinsic dimension deals with non-denumerable infinite sets of properties, it has the highest value. The extrinsic dimension deals with things that potentially have *nearly* (but never quite) infinite properties and, therefore, has less value than the intrinsic dimension. Finally, the systemic dimension, which deals with things dualistically, has the least value of all. We can now see that there is a mathematical hierarchy, wherein the three primary dimensions of value have a natural, objective, universal order:

Dimension	Properties	Value
Intrinsic	Infinite	Highest – Infinite
Extrinsic	Limited	Lesser – Comparable
Systemic	Is / is not	Least – Dualistic

If you wish to optimize value, it is important to think and make value judgments in the proper hierarchical order. Let's look at some specific examples of items in their axiological order and consider the ramifications of ordering them incorrectly.

Dimension	Example	Value
Intrinsic	Caring for Others	Highest – Infinite
Extrinsic	Donating to Charity	Lesser – Comparable
Systemic	Being a particular nationality	Least – Dualistic

Care for people first, then donate to charity, and then be patriotic.

How many people care more about protective patriotism and self-serving politics than about helping to feed starving children in other countries? How many people will give money to charities to soothe a guilty conscience, to get a tax-deduction, or to make the fundraisers go away, yet won't lend a hand to an old woman struggling with her grocery bags? Do these questions sound judgmental? The axiological *fact* is that caring for others *is* an act of higher value than simply donating money to charity, and patriotism and politics *are* of less value than supporting charitable works and providing care and support to others.

Dimension	Example	Value
Intrinsic	An innocent child	Highest – Infinite
Extrinsic	A good job	Lesser – Comparable
Systemic	Private club membership	Least – Dualistic

A child is worth more than your job,
which is worth more than being a member of a club.

Can you imagine being the child of someone who cares more about his or her job, power, prestige, or making money than about you? Sadly, too many people *can* imagine it because they've lived it.

Look at the chart below. Think about what would happen if someone valued these items in the wrong axiological order.

Dimension	Example	Value
Intrinsic	Compassion	Highest – Infinite
Extrinsic	Looking good	Lesser – Comparable
Systemic	Winning a game	Least – Dualistic

To help you get clearer on the potential problems of making poor value judgments, you may want to take a few moments now to write down your thoughts about the potential implications of valuing the above items in the wrong axiological order.

You may already have a sense that our 12,000 to 50,000 thoughts each day are a bit more complicated than just three kinds of thinking/valuing. Once again, we can turn to Dr. Hartman's genius to make sense of the complex way in which we value things in our lives.

Let's look at a simple example: Grandma's antique rocker. It has been in your family for generations. Grandma nursed your mom or dad in that rocker. Your parents nursed you, and you nursed your kids, in that rocker. The chair is very well made, well preserved, and has several lifetimes of memories etched into its grain. Being a rocking chair, it is an extrinsic thing. To the degree that it fulfills the definition and function of a rocking chair, it has extrinsic value. As both an antique and a functional rocking chair, it may also have some monetary value, which is also an extrinsic valuation.

As an heirloom, we can give intrinsic value to the rocker because of the fond memories it holds and the sense of family, belonging, and history it elicits. While a different rocking chair could serve the same functional purpose, no other rocking chair in existence could intrinsically replace Grandma's old chair (and all it means to you). Even if one of the glides was broken and it no longer rocked, it would retain the intrinsic value you gave it. However, if you decided to redecorate your home with high-tech metallic and glass furniture, the rocker may no longer conform to the décor (systemic) and, therefore, it would lose some of its systemic value.

Notice that in the previous example, depending on the *perspective* from which you choose to view the rocking chair (intrinsically, extrinsically, or systemically), it may have more or less value to you.

Now consider a professional football player. What are some of the most basic attributes or properties he would need to be a good football player? He would have to be able to run well, catch well, have sufficient stamina, and know the game. These are extrinsic properties. Now, what happens if he loses both legs in a car accident? Would he now have the properties of—or the realistic potential to be—a good football player? Probably not. *Intrinsically*, however, he still has infinite value as a human being (because he *is* a human being and still has infinite potential value), but he would no longer be able to fulfill at least one of the extrinsic properties of a good football player—someone who can run. Therefore, his extrinsic value *as a football player* would be diminished (but perhaps he could be a great coach!).

Not only can everything be *categorized* as intrinsic, extrinsic, or systemic, all things can *have* intrinsic, extrinsic, and systemic properties. Moreover, all things can be *valued and/or disvalued* intrinsically, extrinsically, and systemically. (You might want to read this paragraph several times to let it sink in.)

Below are some items, along with examples of some of the axiological properties that each item might have. As you read the items and properties, imagine how good you might feel about each item.

Your spouse

Intrinsic: comforting, healing
Extrinsic: good cook, cleans up after themselves
Systemic: always there when I need them, faithful

Your bike

Intrinsic: fond memories: a gift from Dad, joy to ride
Extrinsic: red, 12-speed, good tires
Systemic: freedom to go anywhere, makes me "cool"

Your dog

Intrinsic: the dog I love, gives unconditional love
Extrinsic: playful, fetches well, doesn't shed too much
Systemic: obedient, housebroken

Your boss

Intrinsic: human being
Extrinsic: knows his/her "stuff"
Systemic: listens to all my ideas

This book

Intrinsic: can't put it down, life changing

Extrinsic: nice cover, easy to read print

Systemic: educational and accurate

Now go back and review the above items and properties again, but this time imagine that some of the properties are missing or are qualitatively opposite ("bad"). Would you feel differently about each item? For example, would you still be reading this book if it didn't have enough of the properties of a good book? (You are still reading, aren't you?) What if your boss didn't listen to you at all? How would it impact you if your spouse was unfaithful, your bike had a flat tire, and your dog didn't love you anymore? (You could write a country western song!)

When determining the value of something, it is important to note that its total value is a composite, or "net value," of the positive and negative properties it has in all three dimensions. To know the net value of something, you have to be able to recognize what properties it needs to be a good, whether or not it has those properties, and whether or not it has any "bad" properties that detract from its value.

For example, a thing can have some good properties and some bad properties but still, in the net, be "good enough" and valuable.

• • •

Heart, Hand, and Head

Lead with the heart, lend a hand, and keep your head together.

Metaphor and symbolism can be powerful tools for both learning and understanding. We invite you to think about the three primary dimensions of value symbolically; as the heart, the hand, and the head.

The *Heart* represents the intrinsic dimension. It has the highest value of all. When you let your heart guide you, when you connect with people heart-to-heart, when you have a good and wise heart, you will be more likely to maximize net value.

The *Hand* represents the extrinsic dimension. It's about the physicality of doing, making, and producing with the resources you have available. It is about the labor of your life and the roles that you have— the things you have a hand in.

The *Head* represents the systemic dimension. It's all about thinking, "putting our heads together," mental constructs, dreaming, creativity, judging right from wrong, man-made laws, social norms, and understanding how things fit together into harmonious, useful systems.

You may have realized that the heart, hand, and head also symbolize the spirit, body, and mind. In addition: 'heart' is about people, 'hand' is about resources and productivity; while 'head' is about rules, policies, and norms. All are important. We cannot survive, or optimize goodness and value, without taking good care of all three in their proper order. The chart below illustrates some of the metaphors and parallel concepts for each of the axiological dimensions.

Dimension	Related Metaphors, Symbols and Concepts				
Intrinsic	Heart	Spirit	People	Who	Be
Extrinsic	Hand	Body	Productivity	What/Where	Do
Systemic	Head	Mind	Policy	How	Have

We always want to connect with people heart-to-heart first. If we don't, there is a good chance that we may never reach the point of working hand-in-hand to truly create greater value. In fact, there is a good chance we will end up going head-to-head in hand-to-hand combat, which will ultimately lead to broken hearts.

"A man who works with his hands is a laborer; a man who works with his hands and his brain is a craftsman; but a man who works with his hands and his brain and his heart is an artist."

~ Louis Nizer

• • •

The Sub-Dimensions of Value

Let's take the formal mathematics of axiology one step further.

By now, you are probably aware that anything and everything can be valued or disvalued *in* and *by* each dimension. In other words, every "thing" that is intrinsic, extrinsic, or systemic can be valued and disvalued based upon its intrinsic, extrinsic, and systemic properties and its ability to fulfill an intention or purpose. (You may want to read that again.)

Mathematically, it works out that there are 18 first-order subdimensions of value.

All the first-order combinations of valuing and disvaluing in each dimension are shown here with their axiological expressions:

The *Intrinsic* valuation of an *Intrinsic* thing (I^I)

The *Intrinsic* disvaluation of an *Intrinsic* thing (I_I)

The *Intrinsic* valuation of an *Extrinsic* thing (E^I)

The *Intrinsic* disvaluation of an *Extrinsic* thing (E_I)

The *Intrinsic* valuation of a *Systemic* thing (S^I)

The *Intrinsic* disvaluation of a *Systemic* thing (S_I)

The *Extrinsic* valuation of an *Intrinsic* thing (I^E)

The *Extrinsic* disvaluation of an *Intrinsic* thing (I_E)

The *Extrinsic* valuation of an *Extrinsic* thing (E^E)

The *Extrinsic* disvaluation of an *Extrinsic* thing (E_E)

The *Extrinsic* valuation of a *Systemic* thing (S^E)

The *Extrinsic* disvaluation of a *Systemic* thing (S_E)

The *Systemic* valuation of an *Intrinsic* thing (I^S)

The *Systemic* disvaluation of an *Intrinsic* thing (I_S)

The *Systemic* valuation of an *Extrinsic* thing (E^S)

The *Systemic* disvaluation of an *Extrinsic* thing (E_S)

The *Systemic* valuation of a *Systemic* thing (S^S)

The *Systemic* disvaluation of a *Systemic* thing (S_S)

> Dr. Hartman used exponential expressions (superscripts and sub-scripts) to represent the various sub-dimensions. So, for example, an intrinsic valuation of an intrinsic thing is represented by I^I (spoken as "I to the I"). Similarly, the axiological expression of an intrinsic *disval*-uation of an intrinsic thing is represented as I_I (spoken as "I sub I"). Don't be too concerned about knowing all this; it's provided here for informational purposes only.

You don't need to know the mathematics, or even the 18 sub-dimensions to apply the principles of Axiogenics in your life. However, we do hope that knowing there is sound science behind it will give you the confidence to apply these principles in your life.

• • •

The Hierarchy of Value

Everything in the universe, tangible and intangible, falls somewhere along an objective, mathematical Hierarchy of Value from infinite positive to infinite negative.

> "From the intrinsic evidence of his creation, the Great Architect of the Universe now begins to appear as a pure mathematician."
>
> ~ James Jeans

Since the primary value dimensions are defined mathematically, Dr. Hartman applied mathematics to each of the sub-dimensions. In so doing, he proved that the 18 sub-dimensions also have a *natural and absolute* hierarchy from the most value (significance) to the least. This is what we call the *Hierarchy of Value.*

Mathematically, valuing and disvaluing in the same dimension are of equal absolute significance (e.g., E^I and E_I are equally significant, as are -5 and +5).

The sub-dimensions with the highest significance are the intrinsic valuation of the intrinsic (I^I) and the intrinsic disvaluation of the intrinsic (I_I). In other words, love (I^I) and hate/indifference (I_I) are of equal, mathematically-infinite *significance*. However, love is "better" than hate because love adds to the quality of life (value) while hate takes it away.

Of *least* significance and value are the systemic valuation of a systemic concept (S^S) and the systemic disvaluation of a systemic concept (S_S), such as the right and wrong of "right and wrong."

Say What?

That last one might make your head spin a little bit. This doesn't mean that being right isn't a good thing, only that, in the grand scheme of things and compared to all the other ways of making value judgments, *the right and wrong of things being right or wrong* is of least value.

Clearly "doing the right thing" is a good thing not just because it's right, but more importantly, because the actual right thing creates greater value. If your view of what is right isn't what *actually* creates a greater net value, then being right about it doesn't get you very far.

Don't worry if you're confused or feeling overwhelmed right now. These are some mind-bending concepts and you don't really need to know all the mathematics and axiological meaning to put axiogenic principles to work. Just know that there IS a science-based structure and it works.

Because the Hierarchy of Value is mathematically determined, it is also *universal.* No matter what one believes, or what mathematical system one uses, "infinity" is universally greater than anything less than infinity. Likewise, "many" is universally more than one. Since the Hierarchy of Value is based on a mathematical system, it is also universally true that intrinsic (infinite) value is greater than extrinsic (finite) value, which is greater than systemic (dualistic) value. Being universal, like gravity, the Hierarchy of Value is immutable; it applies at all times, for all people, in all circumstances.

· · ·

Two Domains of Equal Value

There are two parallel Hierarchies of Value.

We can and do make value judgments in each of the 18 sub-dimensions. The next piece of the puzzle is that we also make our value judgments within two broader domains: the *internal domain* and the *external domain.*

The internal domain is all about ourselves—our *Self-View.* It concerns our sense of self worth, our mental constructs about who we are, what our life is about, the roles we play, what motivates us, and the intentions we have for our lives, our roles, and ourselves. It is our sense of how well we fit in the world—our own goodness, our abilities, and our sense of meaning and purpose for our lives. In the internal domain (self-view), we can and do value and disvalue ourselves intrinsically, extrinsically, and systemically.

The external domain—our *World-View*—is about everything outside of our self: all that is beyond the concept of "I." Again, we can and do value and disvalue the world outside of ourselves intrinsically, extrinsically, and systemically.

Thus, we have two domains (internal-self and external-world), each with 18 sub-dimensions: 36 sub-dimensions in total. Each sub-dimension in the internal domain is *axiologically of equal significance* to the *same* sub-dimension in the external domain.

Here are some examples:

- The importance of seeing your own intrinsic value is equal to the importance of seeing the intrinsic value of other people and vice versa.

- Your ability to add value to your own life has equal value to your ability to add value in the world.
- Honoring and appreciating other people's ideas and opinions is just as important as honoring and appreciating your own ideas and opinions.
- Your needs, desires, and priorities have no more or less value than the needs, desires, and priorities of others.

In every case, if you choose one domain over the other, you will limit the total value you could actually create.

• • •

Nature Knows No Right or Wrong

Right and wrong don't exist in Nature.

Axiologically, value itself has no "right" or "wrong"—it simply is. However, we can use axiology to determine "right" and "wrong" from the perspective of that which adds or subtracts value.

Recall the example in Chapter 2 about the boss mulling over the decision to fire someone. We now know that an employee's intrinsic value is always greater than—and distinct from—their extrinsic value. However, job performance is an extrinsic issue—it's what they are hired to do. The boss has a fiduciary responsibility to employ people who can do the job. Still, to maximize net value, the boss must act in a way that upholds the Hierarchy of Value. If the boss ultimately decides to fire the person because they can't, or won't, do their job (which may well be the best decision for the company), the best way to do so, while ensuring integrity with the Hierarchy of Value (maximizing net value for all concerned, including the employee), is to:

- Let him go in a way that does not devalue him intrinsically; honors him as a human being (intrinsic).
- Be honest and clear with the employee about his underperformance (extrinsic).

- Follow the rules, values, and policies of the organization and any applicable labor laws (systemic).

Nature does not care whether or not you fire someone; firing someone, of itself, is neither right nor wrong. The question is, when all things are considered in their proper axiological hierarchy, does it create more value than it takes away?

Axiologically speaking, *there is no right and wrong*, only that which adds value (good) and that which subtracts value (bad). By extension, anything that creates a net loss of value is wrong, while anything that creates a net gain in value is good and right.

• • •

The Axiom of Optimized Value Creation

This simple axiom is the key to humanity's future.

The Hierarchy of Value represents a universal framework for optimizing value judgments and maximizing net value creation. Both mathematically and empirically, all of what we've explored translates into a simple axiom:

We optimize value only when all choices, actions, and reactions are congruent with the Universal Hierarchy of Value.

Any value judgments that are inconsistent with the Hierarchy of Value can potentially, and most often will, result in a net loss of value in some way. Think of it like a car engine. To maximize horsepower and fuel efficiency, while minimizing pollution and operating costs, a car engine needs to be finely tuned (optimized). The sparkplugs need to have just the right spark, and the pistons need to fire in the right order and with proper timing. Any deviation from the optimum will result in some loss of value.

The concept of optimum value creation does *not* suggest a need for laws, legislation, or systems that would attempt to *impose* equal quality of life for all people. Such policies throw a big wrench into the natural process of value creation and ultimately lead to significant reduction in the overall quality of life for everyone. Systems, laws, and policies that artificially limit anyone's potential to create value, could limit the net potential of the whole.

Yet, optimum value creation also requires policies and programs that enable and empower people to discover and unleash their own potential along with rules, laws, and systems that protect their rights to "life, liberty, and the pursuit of happiness."

To prevent intentional or unintentional abuse of power, or the passage of rules and policies that limit potential good, we need checks, balances, and laws that can mitigate these risks.

So clearly, good laws and polices help to optimize value and prevent bad laws, policies, and behaviors from taking it away.

In today's world, we see a number of opposing political philosophies battling for power. At one extreme, we have those who envision a "utopian society" where government policy imposes the distribution of wealth among all people of the society. At the other extreme, we have those who envision a "utopian society" with an every-man-for-himself model of unbridled, competitive free-enterprise, with little or no concern or protection for those who don't have the wherewithal to compete, succeed, or even to survive.

The challenge of governance is to strike a balance that both optimizes and maximizes potential. Axiology shows that the balancing point exists somewhere in the middle—between these opposing philosophies. When leaders have greater clarity and understanding of the laws and principles of value creation, they can approach the task of governance more valuegenically. They can lead and govern in a way that truly unleashes people's collective potential to improve quality of life for themselves, their organizations, and their communities.

> Dr. Hartman understood all this decades ago and dedicated his life to teaching axiological principles to anyone who wanted to learn. He was nominated for the Nobel Peace Prize in 1972 for his pioneering work. Unfortunately, his work was cut short by his passing in 1973.

We must also point out that, even if everyone's thinking were perfectly aligned with the Hierarchy of Value, it does not mean that everyone should or would think the same thing, have the same views, or agree on every possibility. Life is, thankfully, far too variable and complex for that. Because we all have different life experiences, talents, resources, and knowledge, we all bring something different to the table. Axiology simply helps us to sort it all out, to exchange ideas, to learn from each other, and to contribute our own unique gifts to the process of creating a better world.

While, this may be a wonderful ideal and a worthy goal, the practical reality is that virtually no one thinks in complete accordance with the hierarchy of value all the time. In fact, not even most of the time. This is why we need a model to follow *and* a willingness to do the work.

· · ·

Continuous Value Generation

> Axiology provides a universal model for continuous value creation virtually anytime, anywhere, and under any circumstances.

Axiology and the Hierarchy of Value provide a powerful, science-based model for understanding the natural process of value creation. When we understand this model and the underlying principles, we gain important insights into how to apply this process to the effective governance of nation-states, organizations, businesses, and our individual lives.

Based on the premise that the desire for value is driven by the desire to improve quality of life, *quality of life* must be, as Aristotle said, "[the thing] at which all things aim." This being the case, let's explore the relationship between the three primary dimensions of value, how each dimension is served by the next, and how value "flows" between them.

To optimize and maximize value we must apply each value dimension in its proper order and for its proper purpose. The following illustration describes the relationship between the hierarchical value dimensions as well as the spiraling nature of value creation. It is what we call "The Axiological Process of Continuous Value Generation." Study the illustration starting from the top right then follow the arrows in a clockwise direction.

THE AXIOLOGICAL PROCESS OF CONTINUOUS VALUE GENERATION

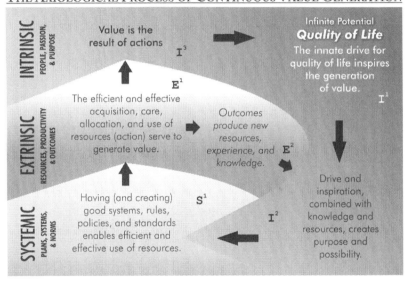

What did you discover? Can you see how the intrinsic, innate desire to improve quality of life drives the process, gives purpose and meaning to our lives, and inspires our goals and possibilities? Can you see how knowledge, insight, experience, and resources allow us to look at how we can create systems that turn possibilities into feasible outcomes? Can you see how everything in the systemic dimension exists to unleash potential and improve the extrinsic dimension? Then, everything that exists in the extrinsic dimension ultimately serves to unleash potential and improve the intrinsic dimension (quality of life)?

The model illustrates how value self-perpetuates. It is a spiraling, evolutionary process. Greater value begets greater value. When this process is followed, everything works towards improving quality of life. As quality of life is improved, more potential is unleashed, creating even more value, which improves quality of life, yet again. When a violation of the Hierarchy of Value interrupts this process, the natural result is a loss of value.

What are the implications of this model for your life and work? For one, this model illustrates the process by which unlimited potential can be unleashed. Second, it reveals why people fail to create greater value and why they may sometime inadvertently destroy value; *any* deviation from this model carries a significant risk of reducing value.

Do you live your life in accordance with this model—this natural process by which humankind actually creates value? To whatever degree you don't, the primary reason is likely to be what we call *value distortions*, which often limit the value you can create and experience.

. . .

Value Distortions

A value distortion is created when a sub-dimension of the Hierarchy of Value is either overvalued or undervalued.

Clearly, we don't all optimize value all the time. Primarily, because somewhere in our personal value hierarchy (value structure), we have some way of looking at things that causes us to make misjudgments of value. Remember, our value structure is formulated from and throughout all of our life experiences: very few of us were taught to think and make decisions based on the Hierarchy of Value. Our culture, society, family, religious institutions, schools, and media have inundated us with thoughts and ideas that often have not supported the development of perspectives, mental habits, and "programs" that are congruent with the universal Hierarchy of Value.

Because we live in an imperfect world, virtually everyone's value structure contains elements that both overvalue and undervalue specific sub-dimension within the Hierarchy of Value. Our over and under valuations create *distortions* in our value judgments whereby we perceive some things as having more or less value than they actually have.

When you overvalue one sub-dimension in the Hierarchy of Value, you must undervalue another. Such *value distortions* can unknowingly cause errors in our value perceptions, throw us off balance, and cause further misinterpretations. As a result, through trial and error, we are continuously compensating and adjusting for these distortions in one situation after another—unwittingly winding and wobbling our way through life.

Inaccurate value judgments within and across the two domains can often either conflict with each other (creating confusion), or feed off each other (creating collusion). Here are some examples:

- An overvaluation of personal satisfaction (internal domain) combined with an undervaluation of rules and norms (external domain) can result in a reduced capacity to set good priorities.
- An overvaluation of one's own ideas (internal domain) combined with an undervaluation of rules and standards (external domain) can create a lack of cooperation and even integrity.
- An overvaluation of one's own ideas (internal domain) combined with an undervaluation of courage and conviction (internal domain) can create what psychologists might call passive-aggressive behaviors.

Here are some other common distortions that can sabotage success and cause a loss of net value:

- When you value having control over making a difference.
- When looking good or being liked takes precedence over being genuine and authentic.
- When you value expedience over following the rules.
- When you value being right more than doing what's right.

What if you could know the exact source of your value distortions and the potential problems that they create? What if you could then learn to eliminate the negative impact of these imbalances? Would it make a difference in your life? Would it eliminate a fair amount of stress, conflict, and even failure in your life?

You know it would.

What if you could know, for sure, what your real and genuine strengths are—where there are no distortions and your value judgments are most clear and accurate? Would you be able to make better choices, take more decisive and effective action, create stronger partnerships, and generate greater success and abundance?

Yes, you would. And yes, you can.

• • •

"The mind is its own place, and in itself
can make heaven of hell."

~ *John Milton,* Paradise Lost

CHAPTER 5

Applied Axiology

"A new way of thinking has become the necessary condition for responsible living and acting. If we maintain obsolete values and beliefs, a fragmented consciousness and self-centered spirit, we will continue to hold onto outdated goals and behaviors."

~ *The Dalai Lama*

The Real Value of Value Science

Using axiology, we can generate greater value out of all other sciences and philosophies and, at the same time, honor and unleash the greatness of the human spirit and the goodness of innate human values.

Many people believe that personal value structures cannot be intentionally changed: that we cannot "teach an old dog new tricks." Of course, many people also believed that man would never fly, when all we needed to do was figure out the principles of physics.

In the 1960's, in what would become Dr. Hartman's post-mortem autobiography, *Freedom to Live: the Robert Hartman Story*, he wrote:

> *"When one reflects that more human beings have been killed by other human beings in this century than in all recorded history, it is not hard to conclude that some things have gone wrong. The diagnosis [sic] is . . . a lack of moral values. We cannot afford any more as could earlier ages, to be bad; that is to invite annihilation. Peace and cooperation have now become pragmatic necessities for man's survival, and this calls for reformation. Humanity, I believe, has never been in such dire need of a science which, by attuning us to moral values as sensitively as we are attuned to technological and material values, can spark that revolution.*
>
> *"For the first time in history, I believe, such a system is possible. For the first time, I feel, scientific knowledge and mastery of the physical nature can be matched by scientific knowledge and mastery of our moral nature. Natural science has changed the world; value science, too, once it is known, developed, and applied, is bound to change the world."[31]*

Unfortunately, not much has changed in the 50-some years since Dr. Hartman wrote those words. Technology continues to flourish and

---

[31] (R. S. Hartman, Freedom to Live: The Robert Hartman Story 1994, 58)

global commerce abounds, yet many in power are all but ignoring the plight of too many of our fellow human beings.

In 1977, Dr. George E. Pugh[32], in one of the seminal literary works regarding the neuroscience behind the value-based systems of the human brain, wrote:

> *"Human values provide the guiding criteria for all personal decisions. They are therefore the fundamental driving force of human history. If we wish to achieve any real changes in either the momentum of history or the trend of our personal lives, we should probably begin with a reevaluation of basic value priorities. The whole structure of modern society is the result of an accumulation of human decisions. It is therefore a reflection of our historical value commitments. To improve our ability to make decisions in a changing environment we need a better understanding of those basic human values that determine what is 'desirable' and what is 'right.'*
>
> *"The need for a better understanding of human values has probably never been more acute than at present, in our rapidly changing society."*

Consider the recent lack of good judgment on the part of a relative few that sent the world economy into a nosedive. Yet we, the people, in our own self-interests or perceived powerlessness, have collectively allowed it to happen. Unfortunately, we have not stood up united in sufficient numbers for the good that we can create and become.

We are concerned that our educational system, in the interest of "political correctness," has shied away from teaching basic human values and the intrinsic skills of life (e.g., interpersonal relationships, communications, teamwork, ethics, the arts, etc.). It seems that we are producing generation after generation with ever-increasing distortions in their value structure. Materialistic values are being rationalized and exaggerated, while human and spiritual values are largely being ignored or even suppressed. So many of our most basic human Values (such as respect,

---

[32] (Pugh 1977)

integrity, personal responsibility, kindness, accountability, and steward-ship) are being lost and, unless we can turn the tide around, our future seems quite uncertain.

Can axiology help us to see a new and more effective path to take? Can the insights gained from neuroscience help us to unleash people's potential for goodness? Can axiology show us the way to a more civil society without treading into the murky waters of moral agendas, philo-sophical arrogance, or religious superiority?

Can we find a way to make this shift simple, practical, and afforda-ble? Could almost anyone, regardless of socio-economic status, but with a reasonable desire and commitment, learn how to use these principles to improve the quality of their life?

Can we do all this and still honor and celebrate our diverse cultural and religious heritage? Yes! Yes! Yes!

. . .

The Universality of Axiological Science

The Laws of Value and The Hierarchy of Value are Universal

Based in logic and mathematics, the Hierarchy of Value and the dy-namics of value creation are as universal as any other law of nature. As such, they could rightly be called the *Natural Laws of Value*. Natural laws provide consistent measurability and predictability.

Axiology is NOT about imposing any particular value or set of Val-ues. It is only about measuring, discerning, and recognizing value. Axiology simply identifies the natural structure and order of the value of things, and helps us to understand the principles and dynamics of Nature that govern the creation and destruction of value. This is no different than how the natural laws of physics govern the dynamics of matter and energy.

Whether you believe in the laws of physics or not, you either act in accordance with them or you suffer the consequences. Similarly, whether you believe in axiology and the Hierarchy of Value or not, you still will either thrive or suffer according to the value choices you make.

Over the years, axiologists have worked with thousands of people and trained hundreds of coaches and consultants in the field of axiology. These coaches and consultants, in turn, have collectively worked with several thousands more people around the world and have spent decades observing natural and social phenomenon. In all of that work and observation, we can unequivocally say that we have yet to discover a single situation in which the laws of value do not apply.

Most of our social norms, human Values, and man-made laws naturally align with the Hierarchy of Value. For example, to steal another person's car is illegal, socially unacceptable, immoral, and out of sync with the natural order of the hierarchy.

Of course, not all laws have been consistent with the Hierarchy of Value. Making it illegal for women or minorities to vote, for example, is a violation of the natural order because it would intrinsically disvalue a group of human beings based on arbitrary extrinsic properties.

The validity of the Hierarchy of Value extends far beyond the *laws* of man. A desire to have my way (systemic) at the expense of your well-being (intrinsic) is a violation of the Natural Laws of Value (let alone, potentially, the Laws of Man) and naturally creates a loss of net value. A failure to make efficient and effective use of resources creates waste and limits abundance. A desire to make money or to get something done (extrinsic) *is* of lesser value than your life, your happiness, love, compassion, or anything else intrinsic. To think that making more money or getting more done is a *requirement* for greater happiness is a value distortion: we all know of people with plenty of money and very little happiness.

Axiology provides a clear and universal model for value creation at every level of life. The model does not only apply on a macro scale (the "big picture" of life), it applies to all the little micro-details of everyday life. It applies to every moment, from the time you awake to the time you go to sleep; from the day you are born to the day you pass on.

As long as you're here—awake and alive—you might as well learn to make the most of it. The following chapters will teach you how.

• • •

The Hartman Value Profile

If you think assessments have little value, think again!

Dr. Hartman believed that if we could measure the degree to which a person's thinking is aligned with the Hierarchy of Value then we could understand how they think. We could understand *why* a person behaves the way they do and even predict how they might behave in the future. He believed that such a measuring tool would be quite valuable for a wide number of applications.

After decades of work and development, Dr. Hartman created a scientifically-validated[33] assessment to do exactly that. It's called the *Hartman Value Profile (HVP)*. Specifically, the HVP directly identifies an individual's current personal value hierarchy with amazing accuracy.

Like an MRI or a CAT scan, the HVP only measures the *current* condition. Our value structures can and do change throughout life, just as our knowledge, perceptions, intentions, goals, and desires change. Because the HVP measures *current* value structures, it can also be used to measure changes over time.

The HVP is nothing like well-known, inductive behavioral and personality assessments, such as Myers-Briggs and DISC. What the HVP measures, as well as its form and methodology, is unique. One inherent problem with most personality and behavior assessments is that they tend to label people as belonging to collective categories, minimizing their individuality. Unfortunately, these labels often become either convenient excuses (for bad behavior) or life sentences ("it's who I am") from which the person can see little escape. Another inherent problem with inductive assessments is that they rely on self-reporting.

---

[33] See http://www.hartmaninstitute.org for information regarding validation studies

This carries the risk of subjective interference or self *mis*-reporting. Several things can cause mis-reporting: an honest misperception of self, a dishonest self-deception (not wanting to admit to themselves what they know to be true), or even intentional deception (wanting to manipulate the assessment results). For these reasons, inductive assessment results can often be misleading or even inaccurate.

Unlike inductive assessments, the *deductive, objective* methodology of the HVP virtually eliminates the risk of subjective interference. The assessment methodology is not a questionnaire like most personality and behavioral assessments. The methodology of the HVP is that the assessment taker rank orders two sets of 18 specific phrases or statements according to the value and meaning they see in the words. Each statement is the linguistic equivalent of an axiological mathematic expression. It is quite interesting to note that there are 6.4 quadrillion[34] different ways to rank each of these two sets of phrases. The Hartman Value Profile has been extensively validated through scientific studies for more than 50 years.[35]

The HVP assesses one's *current* personal value hierarchy or value structure. It identifies and measures *how a person thinks*, rather than their personality or behaviors.

Your personal value hierarchy is the result of all your life experiences, and even genetics may play a role. Because life provides a constant stream of experiences, your personal value hierarchy can and does change throughout life. Behaviors are simply the outward expression, or "acting out," of one's value structure in response to life's conditions and events. These behaviors are based on, and perceived through, the perspectives created by their unique value structure.

The HVP does not measure things like knowledge, life experience, education, intelligence, talent, interests, financial resources, how lucky someone is, or who someone knows. Even so, the combination of a

---

[34] Factorial of 18 or 6,402,373,705,728,000 to be exact.
[35] http://www.hartmaninstitute.org/ValidityStudies/tabid/63/Default.aspx (10/27/09)

person's attributes, resources, and experiences affects their value structure and the perspectives from which they view the world and themselves. So, while a person may draw upon these resources in pursuit of success, if these resources are not valued and applied in a way that is in alignment with the Hierarchy of Value, they may be wasted, misused, or even abused.

. . .

VQ: Value-judgment intelligence quotients

VQ is the objective measure of one's perceptive ability to make value judgments from each of the 36 axiological perspectives.

"What is life but the angle of vision? A man is measured by the angle at which he looks at objects. This is his fate and his employer."

~ Ralph Waldo Emerson

Think of each of the 36 axiological sub-dimensions as unique *perspectives* from which you can assess or make value judgments about something or someone. In other words, each sub-dimension represents an *axiological value perspective* from which we can make a value judgment. In common usage, "perspective" means a "point of view"—a position from which we view, assess, and value things.

Axiological Perspectives

For example, you can view/value a person from an extrinsic *perspective*. You can assess their extrinsic attributes (e.g., how their appearance, skills, and experience might add or subtract from their ability to do a job). Of course you can also view/value people intrinsically (Do we love them? Do we see their unique value?) or systemically (Do we agree with what they think?).

As we said in a previous section, value distortions, within and across domains and sub-dimensions, can cause challenges. These distortions are the result of misperceptions of value. Perception is a function of perspective. You have the power to shift your perspective. If you could know which perspective provides you with the clearest perception of value, you would be able to choose that perspective and, therefore, make better value judgments.

The Measurement of VQ

> "If you can measure it, you can improve it."
>
> ~ Paraphrasing Lord Kelvin (William Thomson)

Your VQ (Value-judgment intelligence Quotient) is the objective scoring of your capacity to perceive and judge value from each of the 36 axiological perspectives using the HVP. Your VQ profile consists of all 36 measurements (VQ scores).

High-VQ scores indicate high levels of perceptive ability, thus a capacity to make good value judgments. These are your most valuegenic capacities because they most support your ability to make good value judgments. Low-VQ scores indicate lower levels of perceptive ability, thus a diminished capacity to make good value judgments.

A VQ score also identifies whether a specific perspective is overvalued or undervalued. If you to put too much or too little value on something, you are, by definition, making an inaccurate value judgment. Whenever you overvalue or undervalue one perspective, it is always at the expense of another. For example, if you undervalue people's intrinsic value, it is because you are overvaluing something else.

Each low-VQ perspective has specific associated risks—potential perceptions, choices, and behaviors that reduce value in one or more aspects of life. Additionally, the associated risks are different, depending on whether the perspective is overvalued or undervalued.

Higher-VQ perspectives have the potential to produce clearer, more accurate value judgments. They support positive personality characteristics, choices, and behaviors. High VQs also have the potential to reduce or even prevent stress, upset, and conflict.

Whether or not you know your VQ profile, its affect is real; it is a representation of your unique personal value structure.

• • •

You and Your VQ Profile

Your VQ affects all of your choices, actions and reactions.

Virtually everyone has some VQ scores that are brilliant, highly perceptive and accurate (high VQs) and others that are challenged one way or another (low VQs). Unfortunately, all too often, it is our lower-VQ perspectives that have the greatest influence on our thoughts, choices, and decisions, whether they are serving us well or not.

Left to our automatic habits of mind, we will *always* act and react in accordance with our most dominant perspectives. When a low-VQ perspective is running the show, we are likely to follow its lead automatically, gaining whatever benefits it might provide, but also having to suffer its consequences.

A habit of placing a high value on seeing new possibilities may well give us the drive and determination to turn a dream into reality. However, such a habit can also keep us so focused on accomplishment that it may be difficult to focus on other responsibilities and relationships. It can even prevent us from simply being in the now; enjoying the moment and basking in the company and comfort of others.

Because mental habits take less energy and are automatically triggered, they tend to run the show when we let them. In terms of the *power of influence* that our VQs have over us, our strengths (high VQs) are often weak and our weaknesses (low VQs) are often strong. In other words, our weaknesses are "bad" mental habits tend to dominate.

Axiologically, a "bad" habit is simply a habit or thought process that does not have *all* the properties needed to fulfill our purpose of maximizing net value. "Bad" habits of mind are really just habitual, automatic perceptive tendencies that have a low VQ, where our perception is "weak" or limited and do not fully support success in *all* areas of life.

Our value judgments, good or bad, show up in our choices, decisions, behaviors, attitudes, actions, and reactions.

Do you know people who habitually focus on what's wrong with others, look at things with a pessimistic eye, or are so concerned about being right that they have to make others wrong? How about perfectionists, procrastinators, complainers, or blamers? Chances are, you also know people who are upbeat and positive, are open and caring of others, or seem highly accountable and responsible.

What vs. Why

While it is easy to observe behaviors and "personality" traits, it is not so easy to know *why* people do what they do or think what they think without knowing their VQ profile.

We have found, for example, that a low VQ pertaining to self-respect may cause a person to feel a need to put up a façade. They worry that if they don't "look" positive and upbeat, people will find out that they're not really "good enough." An observer, however, even their close friends and family, may falsely assume that their self-esteem is good.

An overvaluation of perfection—"if I can't do it right, I won't do it at all"—can easily drive procrastination. An undervaluation of the benefits of getting "the little things" done, or even an overvaluation of doing only "fun and exciting things," can also cause procrastination.

Here's another example: imagine that you are trying to make a decision about a new car purchase. How would you go about it? You could look at it systemically: what kind of car will serve my purpose (sedan, truck, van, two-door, four-door, etc.)? You could look at it extrinsically: how well is it made, how much does it cost, how reliable will it be, how fuel-efficient is it, and how cool does it look? You could also look at it intrinsically: how will I feel when I'm driving it? All of these could go into our decision making process, and all of these are specific axiological perspectives in which your VQ could be very high or very low.

If your VQ is low in any perspective that may be involved in buying the car, it may diminish your capacity to make a good buying decision.

What's more, if the salesperson is good at exploiting your low VQs, you could easily be swayed into making an even worse decision or coerced into buying add-ons you don't really need or want.

For some people, one or more low VQs may be irrelevant if their life-circumstances don't trigger the associated issues. For example, someone who rarely interacts with other people at work may have little need for the VQ measurements associated with interacting with other people. But, this low VQ could cause a problem in their personal life. If they are a loner in their personal life, then it may not be an issue on a daily basis. Of course, it's also quite possible that a low VQ for relating to "people" is precisely *why* they have designed their life the way they have; so they don't have to deal with people.

Almost everyone has several high-VQ perspectives that could virtually eliminate the challenges coming from any low-VQ perspective if they are willing and able to look at things from a different perspective. If they *shifted their perspective to one with a higher VQ*, then they would see things quite differently. As a result, they could make different and, most likely, better choices.

By all accounts, Cindi is a kind and wonderful person. People love her positive attitude and the way she always points out the good in other people. She is professionally successful and financially secure; but when I met her, her love-life was a mess. For years, she had repeatedly fallen in love with men who treated her rather poorly.

Her VQ profile indicated that she overvalued the good extrinsic attributes of people. Although her VQ profile supported her in seeing the potential good in people, she was often "blinded by love" to the negative attributes of the men she was attracted to. Even when her intuition told her something was "off," she would find ways to justify the relationship.

Her VQ for courage and conviction was low and undervalued. As a result, she seemed to justify the situation by believing she could tolerate the abuse until they would somehow "come around" (which they never did). After all, she had grown wiser, so why couldn't they? Consistently, her relationships would fall apart when either she couldn't take the abuse any more or the man would get tired of her and look for "greener pastures" elsewhere.

When Cindi first started the coaching, she was dazed and confused. She had just escaped from her latest "nightmare." Even though she felt he had emotionally abused her spirit, and cheated in their relationship, she couldn't help but see and defend all the potential good in him. She had started to believe that something must be wrong with *her;* otherwise, why would "every" man she likes treat her this way?

By the end of her four months of coaching, she was clear that her "problem" was not just her choice in men, but also the choices she made about *herself*, which drove her to make poor choices in men. What she discovered about herself helped her recover her sense of worthiness, discover her strengths, and begin to build a foundation for an extraordinary partnership with "the man of her dreams," whoever he may be.

Months later, she called and said that she had found him—"the man of her dreams." He wanted to do his VQ assessment. The assessment results revealed it was a 'match made in heaven!'

Life is often complicated, so it is generally useful to view circumstances, situations, or options from multiple perspectives before making a choice or taking an action. This helps to ensure that the choice, action, or reaction is the best it can be. Considering that it is our lower VQs that tend to attract our attention, it's important that we make the conscious effort to look at things from our higher-VQ perspectives so we can see the full picture and then make better choices.

As said earlier, most people have much more perceptive ability than they ever fully utilize. Being "attracted" to old, less helpful, lower-VQ perspectives is NOT a function of any personality flaw, only a function of not having learned to shift our perspective to leverage the existing strengths of our higher VQs.

. . .

A Question of Balance

Your low VQs are not all bad. In fact, they may be exactly what is driving you to certain forms of success and driving you "nuts" at the same time.

Low VQs are not always problematic. In some circumstances, a low VQ can actually serve to drive a person to do things they wouldn't otherwise do. In fact, almost any low VQ can have a potential upside. However, low VQs usually do come at a price. The question is, what's the price? Can you take advantage of the upside without having to suffer the cost?

We've assessed several hundred highly successful business people, including self-made millionaires. Interestingly, some of them have a lower overall VQ than you might expect. This may cause one to wonder if all this talk about the importance of having a high VQ is just a bunch of hogwash. It's not.

Success comes in many forms. Low VQs can drive success in one area of life (e.g., business) and limit success in another (e.g., personal relationships) or vice versa.

Real success is about optimizing the richness of goodness and value in *all* aspects of your life. What value is money, if you have no loved one's to enjoy it with? What value is fame, if your children despise you? What value is power, if you are powerless to be with a loved one in their time of greatest need? On the other hand, if you get so concerned about your family, neighbors, or community that you do not have the time or energy to make a living or take good care of yourself, you may have a different set of problems to deal with.

All of these examples are the result of one or more low-VQ perspectives that cause us to value something either higher or lower than its actual axiological value. By definition, a low VQ is a perception that something is or has either greater or lesser value than it actually does.

One way or the other, if you let low VQs run your life, you run the risk of throwing your life out of balance and missing out on important parts of what makes life worthwhile.

The goal is to make your strengths stronger and your weaknesses weaker (again, in terms of their influence). Doing this requires a sufficient level of conscious self-awareness where you are not simply running on automatic; letting your low-VQ habits run the show. It's also not about giving up what's good about a habit or a low VQ; it's about maximizing the good in *all* your thoughts and habits.

You want to learn how to recognize when a low VQ is dominating your thoughts and to consciously shift your thinking to a higher-VQ perspective. This allows will allow you to maximize your potential for answering The Central Question in a way that maximizes value creation and minimizes any negative risks associated with low-VQ thinking alone. With proper practice, you can learn to use more of the good aspects of both high and low VQs. You can make the most of what you *already* have and make it better.

Using the example of turning a dream into reality, the goal is to work towards a possibility *and* enjoy each moment at the same time. Whether your focus is on making money, raising a family, providing retirement security, personal or spiritual growth, gaining power or fame, or just having fun, the purpose is to create greater value and improve your quality of life. The more you put valuegenic principles to work in your life, the faster you will become more valuegenic and develop new strength-focused, "good" habits of mind that can improve every area of your life.

· · ·

Applications of VQ Profiling

There is virtually no aspect of life in which VQ cannot or does not play a fundamental role.

The ability to measure VQ allows us to identify and quantify the often hidden, under-utilized strengths and risk-laden challenges in people's thinking habits and to predict behavioral tendencies with amazing accuracy. More importantly, we are able to help people understand why they think and act the way they do and how, if they so desire, they can change. By engaging in axiogenic principles, people can create positive, organic changes in the neuropathways of their brain so that the change is genuine and authentic as opposed to faked, forced, or based in mere self-deception.

Measuring VQ also allows us to assess how well someone is likely to perform in almost any situation. We can measure their capacity to answer The Central Question accurately. This can be particularly valuable when you are trying to decide whom to hire, promote, invest in, or even marry.

Here are just a few examples of areas in which we can, and have, applied this technology:

- Developing executive leadership and management talent
- Enhancing organizational development initiatives
- Facilitating change, reorganizations, and mergers
- Assessing candidates for hire and promotion
- Working with business investors (VCs and Angels) to assess leadership teams before and after they invest
- Benchmarking critical performance factors for specific roles and responsibilities
- Building healthy relationships and partnerships
- Parenting and family dynamics
- Engaging people in personal growth and development
- Dealing with the challenges of stress, addictions, and criminal recidivism

- Improving public education
- And many more . . .

We believe that Axiogenics could also have a dramatic impact on a number of psychological conditions, such as post-traumatic stress, bipolar disorder, and certain forms of depression. Psychologist, Dr. Leon Pomeroy writes, "A new breed of psychologist is now required, one having value-centric cognitive sensitivities to recognize the potential of Hartman's work, plus the initiative to bring it into psychological research and practice."[36]

• • •

Discover Your VQ Today

Don't guess. Assess.

We invite you take the Axiogenics VQ Profile assessment now. It's free. It only takes about 20 minutes to complete. Once you complete the assessment, you will immediately receive an introductory report (via email) that will show you some of your most significant VQ scores.

Your introductory report will give a personalized context for the upcoming chapters in which we will reveal the practices for becoming more valuegenic. Not only will you have the opportunity to *read about* how to use your strengths, but also you'll be able to start *applying* the practices we describe for making better use of your primary strengths and reducing the impact of your lowest VQs. Before you even finish reading this book, you could be seeing some real results in your life or work, and probably both.

If you would like to take the assessment now, just go to:

http://www.VQProfile.com/book

---

[36] (Pomeroy 2005)

CHAPTER 6

Axiogenics –
Applied Neuro-Axiology

"When subjective values are conceived to have objective consequences in the brain, they no longer need to be set off in a realm outside the domain of science. The old adage that science deals with fact, not with values, and that value judgments lie outside the realm of science no longer applies in the new framework."

~ Roger Sperry

"Just as natural science helps us use the greater of nature, axiological science will help us use the even greater strength of the human spirit to break out of the system that has hypnotized and enslaved us. Then we and our grandchildren will truly have freedom to live."

~ Dr. Robert S. Hartman

Trust and Partnership

Above all else, our relationships with other people have the greatest value and are the greatest source of potential value generation.

You know from the Hierarchy of Value that people have the highest intrinsic value. By extension, then, the relationships we have with people also have much greater potential value than anything else. This potential value is unleashed when the individuals in a relationship are not hampered by their own low-VQ fears, concerns, agendas, and self-imposed limits, or by the low-VQ impositions of others.

Partnership is about relating to one another in ways that unleash the valuegenic potential in each person. Unleashing potential requires mutual trust. Perhaps the greatest tragedy of human history has been our tendency to limit each other's potential, which destroys trust. To reach our own potential we must allow and encourage others to reach theirs. Potential is not additive, it is exponential. Your potential is multiplied by other people's potential and vice versa.

Personal growth, intimacy, vulnerability, trying new things, creativity, and letting go of fears and attachments are all fraught with risks. Too often, the perceived risks are greater than the perceived gains. Yet, it's only when people are willing to risk going beyond the edge of their comfort zone, that their potential can be transformed into reality.

Our fear of risk emanates from a perception that we may be harmed or disvalued in some way—this is what makes risk risky. People need to know that it's ok to risk; that they will not be intrinsically disvalued when they take a risk, regardless of the outcome. The essence of trust is knowing that you are safe in the hands of another; that you will not be disvalued or harmed. Trust eliminates a great deal of the fear and riskiness associated with risk.

In the absence of trust, people hold back their potential, but in the presence of trust, they will unleash it. In a trusting partnership, the partners are willing to hold each other accountable (in a valuegenic way) and to be held accountable. They are each willing to learn and grow from their failures and misjudgments without feeling a need to self-protectively defend and justify themselves.

Can you imagine how the quality of a relationship would improve if partners began asking themselves what choice they could make and action they could take, in each moment, to create the greatest net value in the relationship and/or for the other person?

Of course, it also begs the question: why don't we already do this? The answer is found in the gaps between people's perceptions.

• • •

Gaps: Threats or Opportunities?

Differences in perception, when seen as threats, usually limit our opportunities to optimize axiological value and can also wreak neurological havoc.

We can boil down what stands in the way of greater trust, partnership, and abundance, and what virtually all of our stresses, struggles, and conflicts are about, to one thing—unreconciled gaps.

A "gap" is simply a difference in value perception between two perspectives, or between our perception and reality. If you perceive something one way, I perceive it a different way, and one of us has a problem with the other's perception, there is a good chance that we could end up in a conflict. An *unreconciled* gap is any gap that is causing a problem—a gap that is "not ok" with us.

In a broad sense, there are two kinds of unreconciled gaps: ones we don't know about (unrecognized) and ones we do know about (recognized).

Unrecognized gaps are most often the result of false assumptions, missing information, or unknown differences in perception between two or more people. Clearly, unrecognized gaps can make it much more difficult to answer The Central Question. We can look for gaps or wait until they catch us by surprise; either way, once identified, they become *recognized* gaps.

Not all recognized gaps are a problem. For example, you go to a restaurant with a friend; you order steak and they order seafood. It's probably not a problem that you each wanted something different. The gap doesn't need to be reconciled; there is nothing to reconcile. However, if you wanted to share a bottle of wine, it could pose a problem if you only like red wine and they only like white.

Any gap that is "not ok," is an unreconciled gap. Have you ever argued with someone over what each of you felt was "right?" What really happened was that there was an unreconciled gap between your understanding or opinion and theirs, and it was *not ok* for one or both of you for the gap to exist! An amygdala hijack is a reactive response to an unreconciled gap, usually between an expectation and reality, that is *really not ok with you.*

Low-VQ perspectives tend to cause the mind to see unreconciled gaps as threats. When we see things as threats, the amygdala reacts and we usually end up in stress, upset, or conflict.

In an organization, to the degree that unreconciled gaps exist between people, between departments, or between people and the organization's mission, purpose and culture, there will be dysfunction, ongoing conflict, lost productivity, and diminished performance.

But what if people could view unreconciled gaps, not as threats, but as *opportunities* instead? Like many situations in life, a different perspective can change everything.

As you learned in Chapter 3, when you see things as threats, you will usually have some measure of an amygdala hijack. Your brain then fires off certain bio-chemicals that *limit* your ability to think rationally.

However, when you can see unreconciled gaps as opportunities, your brain behaves very differently. Opportunities feel good because your brain produces bio-chemicals that feel good and *expand* your capacity to think rationally and even intuitively. The synapses and neuropathways that give access to your memories, your logic-centers, and your meaning-making brain-centers, open wider.

Hence, by using The Central Question and other axiogenic practices, you can begin to see things more as opportunities than as threats; you can begin to think in ways that allow you to make better value judgments. You can utilize your high VQs to reduce and eliminate gaps and to reconcile, resolve, or accept at face value whatever gaps you are able to recognize. Simultaneously, you will be engaging in a deliberate practice that causes your brain to be more supportive of your success, rather than less.

Of all the strengths that you could master, and of all the gaps that you could reconcile, it is the strengths and gaps that are relevant to trust and partnership that are most important. As you read the rest of this book, keep the importance of trust and partnership in mind. Make building trust and partnership your first priority in becoming more valuegenic and everything else will fall into place.

• • •

Connecting the Dots

Axiology and neuroscience come together in an amazing dance of harmony and power.

"Humanity has only scratched the surface of its real potential."

~ Peace Pilgrim

Neuroscience is a natural physical science, while axiology (value science) is a non-physical science. Axiology, like psychology, sociology, and economics, is a science that deals with non-physical things. Axiology is the study of how we think, and to think is to value. Thinking and valuing are inseparable from the spiritual and moral elements of goodness and the infinite potential of the human spirit. At the same time, axiology provides a mathematical, observable, and scientifically validated framework for understanding the *natural laws* of value, Values, and valuing. Thus, axiology is both a non-physical *and* a natural science.

In our discussion on neuroscience, you learned that conscious thought requires more energy than sub-conscious habits. Change requires deliberate effort, repetition, and intensity. Change is not always easy, but you can make the journey much easier and less stressful by taking your unique "path of least resistance." Your "path of least resistance" is your high-VQ perspectives.

To create new habits, you must be able to see (perceive) greater potential value in the new habit, *independent* of the old habit, without it being about compensation. Your high VQs are the perspectives from which this happens most naturally. When you choose a higher-VQ perspective, you are NOT giving energy to the old low-VQ habitual perspectives. Thanks to synaptic pruning, the mental muscles (neuropathways) associated with low-VQ perspectives will begin to atrophy. That is, they will lose synaptic connections and thus become "weaker."

Meanwhile, as your old habits atrophy, you are building new habits based on perspectives and capacities that are already aligned with the Hierarchy of Value. This further reduces the risk that a low VQ will interfere with or limit your ability to recognize gaps and optimize value.

When you are being valuegenic (and using your high VQs), you will tend to see gaps as opportunities to create value, rather than threats that may take value away. When you embrace these opportunities, you learn, grow, and build upon your strengths.

Over time, your high VQs will naturally begin to create new connections and "pull" your low VQs into greater alignment with the Hierarchy of Value (raising their overall VQ). We can't scientifically prove it today, but we suspect the mechanics of this have to do with synaptic pruning and how our brains make multiple connections and associations *between* neuropathways. Remember, "What's wired together, fires together." As the synapses (connections) between neurons associated with a low VQ atrophy (weaken) and disappear (from disuse), new synapses take root and connect the neurons to other neurons associated with high VQs. Over time, we develop new habits of mind (neuropathways) that are associated with strengths rather than weaknesses.

What we can prove, with real data, is that overall VQ scores do increase over time when people practice axiogenic principles. We usually assess clients before and after coaching engagements. While the improvement varies from person to person, the average improvement is about 19% after just 3 months of coaching.

Axiogenics is a process for developing a real Midas Touch—the mind-brain alchemy of turning everyday events into the "gold" of greater goodness. Of course saying it is much easier than doing it. So let's look closer at *how* you shift your thinking to be more valuegenic: to develop a higher level of consciousness and self-awareness, to liberate more of the potential in your high-VQ perspectives. Then let's look at how you go about answering The Central Question.

· · ·

Conscience and Auto-Conscience

You already have the power to transcend your old habits and make better use of your strengths.

"The significant problems we face cannot be solved at the same level of thinking we were at when we created them."

~ Albert Einstein

Look back on your own life experiences. Isn't it true that there were times when you knew you were not doing the "right" thing, yet did it anyway? Haven't there been times when you just "couldn't help yourself"? Have you ever been fully aware that you were being vindictive, hard-headed, stubborn, or unreasonably angry, but in the moment, you just didn't care or couldn't stop yourself (i.e., had an amygdala hijack)?

Haven't there been times when, out of frustration or anger, you acted mean or hurtful, but didn't realize it until it was too late and the damage had already been done? How many times have you recognized the "error of your ways," even those stupid little mistakes we all make, only when you look back in hindsight?

All of the above are examples of "running on automatic." Notice that you can be very aware that you are running on automatic, and yet feel powerless to "get control of yourself." This is what we call your *auto-conscience.*

The auto-conscience is all your habitual/automatic ways of perceiving and reacting. To be sure, not all of your perspectives and habits of mind are "bad." Indeed, some, many, or even most of them have been "good enough" to get to where you are today. Still, some could be better and will need to be better to get you where you want to be in the future. Because habits can so dominate our thinking, even one or two low-VQ "bad" habits can wreak devastation and severely limit our success.

With that said, if you are totally unaware of how you are thinking or being in the moment, you are—in that moment—essentially powerless to make any kind of conscious choice about anything.

Unfortunately, as we stated earlier, for most people the auto-conscious mind is dominated by lower VQs. While the theoretical ideal is to have a "perfect VQ" (in which all 36 measurements are maximized), we never measured anyone with such "perfection." If we could achieve such a state, theoretically our auto-conscious mind would consist only of good habits. This, one might say, would be the ultimate goal. Not many people in history have achieved such a state.

For those of us who have not yet reached this level of enlightenment, the task is to develop the self-awareness and presence of mind to recognize when we are in an auto-conscious state, and then to deliberately rise above it to a higher level of consciousness. When you are operating from a state of higher conscience, YOU are "in charge" of your thoughts and have the power and opportunity to shift your perspectives so you can make different and better choices.

What seems apparent is that our "higher conscience" is what drives our fundamental ability to know right from wrong and good from evil, as well as our desire to add value. Many people believe that it is the higher conscience that connects us to the "collective-conscience," to universal intelligence, or to God.

Sometimes, when we really connect with our higher conscience, we experience some of the most magical moments of life: moments of inexplicable clarity, understanding and ease. Some people call it "being in the flow." What's really happening is that your higher conscience is accessing your highest VQs.

Through neuro-axiology, we have discovered an even more direct and deliberate route to this heighted level of clarity. Moreover, through proper practice you can eliminate old, limiting habits and create new, more value-enhancing habits. By becoming valuegenic you can make a habit out of "being in flow." When you consistently ask and accurately answer The Central Question, you naturally propel yourself forward and upward in the value creation process.

Being valuegenic requires a high level of self-awareness: to know your true strengths and weaknesses. It requires the mental muscle and self-discipline to deliberately raise your consciousness and shift your frame of reference to a higher-VQ perspective. When you do, you can better utilize all of the "good" in both your high and low VQs while avoiding, reducing, and even eliminating the potential negative impact of your low VQs.

A key to developing this capacity is to use *Centering Questions*.

• • •

Centering Questions

You have more power than you know. It's just a matter of learning to shift your perspective from low VQs to high VQs.

> "Questions provide the key to unlocking our unlimited potential."
>
> ~ Anthony Robbins

Think of The Central Question as the clutch in car with a manual transmission. You can use it to disengage from a mental gear (VQ perspective) that isn't helping you fulfill your purpose (usually a low VQ). This allows you to shift into one that does (a high VQ).

Centering Questions are like a mental gear-shift. They are used to shift your thinking into a specific high-VQ that can help you answer The Central Question and accelerate your success in adding value. Centering Questions are NOT rhetorical questions. They evoke genuine curiosity and wonderment, and demand an accurate answer.

John knew he had a problem. He had a tendency not to listen and to argue his point without really taking the time to consider or understand other people's point of view. The more he fought, the more people fought back. He could feel it happening to him: his blood pressure would go up, his jaw would tighten, and he would either become aggressive or just clam up. He also knew it was costing him dearly in both his personal and professional relationships.

Another coach had told him that when this happens, he should take a deep breath, count to ten, and if he still didn't feel "under control," he should just walk away. He told me that this wasn't working very well and he felt there had to be a better way, but he just didn't know what it was.

I suggested that the issue wasn't really that he didn't know what to say or how to say it. The real issue had to do with "gaps." He was trying to deal with an unreconciled gap from the perspective of a low VQ. Because low VQs tend to see unreconciled gaps as threats, his brain was reacting defensively. I taught him how to use Centering Questions like, "What is this person feeling right now? What might be good about what they are trying to say? What's important to them?" I taught him to ask these questions of *himself* and to notice how, when his perspective changed, it became less about him, less of a threat, and more about opportunity, curiosity and understanding. I encouraged him to use his Centering Questions as a way for him look at the situation from a different perspective.

In our next coaching session, John shared with me that he was realizing just how strong his need to argue was and he could see that it was being driven by a low VQ. This low VQ had been causing him to value "being right" over finding the best answer.

When he used his Centering Questions, his low-VQ tendencies literally became irrelevant, and in those moments, they no longer had power over him. He began to see everything in life more as an opportunity than a threat, and it changed everything for him.

Over time, several things began to happen for John. First, he stopped getting upset when he didn't get to have his "say." He realized he often didn't need to "say" anything, and he began to listen more and to ask more questions. Rather than battling over unreconciled gaps, he was creating opportunities to create understanding and trust. When he did this, people began to open up, confide, and share ideas with him more often. Whenever he did have something to say, they listened.

For the first time in many years, he was feeling like he mattered; that he was someone who actually made a difference.

As you know, there are three basic axiological perspectives (dimensions): intrinsic, extrinsic, and systemic. Intrinsic Centering Questions are about intrinsic things (people–e.g., What is she feeling? What is unique and irreplaceable? What matters to them?). Extrinsic Centering Questions are about extrinsic things (e.g., What needs to be done right now? What resources are available and what is the best use of them?). Systemic Centering Questions are about systemic things (e.g., What is the value of having and/or following this rule or establishing this policy? What is right? What is wrong?).

The key to making any good decision is to consider your options from as many relevant perspectives as possible. It is always best to use your high-VQ perspectives to increase the odds of making the best possible decisions. Obviously, if you try to consider issues from a low-VQ perspective, not only do you run the risk of making a poorer decision, you are also likely to cause a bit of stress, frustration, and confusion for yourself and, possibly, others. Your low-VQ perspective(s) may even have you convinced you that you are right, even though you haven't yet explored all the relevant issues and options.

When you are thinking outside your areas of strength (low VQs), Centering Questions will "pull" you into your strengths. They shift your point of view to where you have greater clarity: a perspective with a high VQ that will lead you to the best answers. Centering question instantly "fire up" the neuropathways associated with your high VQs.

Shifting your perspective is a process you have used to make many of the good decisions in your life. We all do this at times, though it's not always easy. Each shift in perspective gives you additional insight and, hopefully, greater clarity. By looking at an issue from multiple perspectives, asking yourself (and perhaps others) questions relevant to each perspective, and then making judgments based on your perception, you eventually arrive at a decision. You deliberate and then you decide.

Centering Questions instantly cause you to be more valuegenic by leveraging the power of your high-VQ strengths and minimizing any risk or negative influence of your low-VQ perspectives. When you ask yourself a Centering Question, some very interesting things happen:

- You'll almost instantly start perceiving things differently and gain insights you haven't had before.
- You'll recognize and reconcile more gaps.
- Your stress levels and physiological tensions will dissipate.
- You'll embrace life more and feel threatened less.
- Your aspirations will become nobler, less self-centric, and more achievable.
- You'll procrastinate less, listen more; defend and justify less, trust the universe more; have less self-doubt and more self-confidence.
- You'll instantly improve the quality of your choices and the value that your actions and reactions create. As a result, you'll immediately begin moving closer to achieving your goals and aspirations.

If have taken us up on our offer to take the free VQ assessment, then you already have at least one of your most important sets of Centering Questions. If you haven't, you may want to take it now. We'll be talking more about how to use Centering Questions in just a little bit.

If you don't have your free report yet, The Central Question *can* be used as a "general purpose" Centering Question.

• • •

Strength-Focused Deliberate Practice

You may have the talent (your high VQs) and the intentions (value-centeredness), but talents and intentions alone may not be enough—you have to practice, practice, valuegenic practice!

> "Success is achieved by developing our strengths, not by eliminating our weaknesses"
>
> ~ Marilyn vos Savant

From a VQ perspective, a "weakness" is defined as a reduced capacity to make good value judgments. A low VQ is a perspective from which your perception is not in alignment with the Hierarchy of Value. Low VQs can often cause us to make misjudgments that result in choices and actions that don't create greater net value. Yet, as you learned in Chapter 3, focusing on fixing your weaknesses is a neurological trap.

Your strengths are your high VQs. By definition, they are perspectives that are naturally more aligned with the Hierarchy of Value and, therefore, can support good value judgments. Focusing on strengths not only gives you the immediate benefits of what your strengths can produce, it also allows you to engage the principles of neuroplasticity, which provide important long-term benefits. *Strength-focused* deliberate practice is the key to turning strengths into habits, raising your overall VQ, and increasing your capacity for ever-greater success.

Your high-VQ strengths are also the key to the forth core principle of Axiogenics:

1. Value drives success in all endeavors
2. Your mind-brain is already value-driven
3. There is a universal Hierarchy of Value
4. *Accurately answering The Central Question is the key to maximizing your success.*

In Chapter 3, you were also introduced to the effectiveness of "deliberate practice" to help people develop their talents. In chapters 4 and 5, you learned about the Hierarchy of Value and VQ. When you combine value-centeredness (intentions) with high-VQ strengths, and then repeatedly apply *strength-focused* deliberate practices, the natural result—the virtually *unavoidable* result—is that you become more valuegenic; you find better answers to The Central Question and take action that create greater value and success in your life.

You already have the talents (high-VQ strengths) that can help you more accurately answer The Central Question. Hopefully, you also have the desire and intention. But, are intentions enough?

It is said that the road to hell is paved with good intentions. Indeed, how often have you watched people with the greatest of intentions make a mess of things, but affirm their continued good intentions by saying something like "from now on I'll . . ."? Or, how often have you heard people attempt to make excuses, or deflect blame and responsibility, by claiming that, since their intentions were good, it must not be their fault? How many New Year's resolutions have you made with great intentions, year after year, only to forget all about your intentions by January 15th?

The fact is, an *intention* is just a mental construct about the future. No action is required in order to have an intention. Intention speaks to a future, a dream, a goal, an aspiration, or a desire. Clearly, intentions are important; however, in the absence of effective action, only chance or good luck will cause the intention to be fulfilled.

Unless you want to leave the success of your life, your relationships, or your organization to chance, you must develop mastery of the skills required to deliberately take the actions that will lead to greater success.

Effective action requires a sound foundation upon which to make good action choices. By now, you have an understanding that your high-VQ perspectives *are* the foundation upon which you can begin to make the most effective choices and, therefore, take the most effective actions.

It may come as no surprise that in the world of athletics and performing arts, the proponents of deliberate practice explicitly state that deliberate practice is about *fixing weaknesses*. For example, "conventional wisdom" says that a golfer who struggles with putting needs to "fix" his putting. We now know from neuroscience, however, that when it comes to personal development and the development of *mental habits*, this approach has been misunderstood and misapplied.

In chapter 4, we introduced you to the Process of Continuous Value Generation. You will recall that the process shows that to create greater quality of life, we must have systems that allow us to make the best possible use of our resources.

Your high VQs are your most precious and powerful resources when it comes to answering The Central Question and taking action. Therefore, it makes sense to have a system and method of practice that allows you to make good use of these resources.

What follows is a *strength-focused* deliberate practice for answering The Central Question. This process works anytime, anywhere, under any circumstances when you have the presence of mind to use it. The more you use it, the more it will become a natural habit.

· · ·

Answering The Central Question

> To answer The Central Question to the best of your ability, be SMART about how you approach it.

As we have established, it is your high VQs that have the highest potential to help you accurately answer The Central Question and take actions that generate greater net value. But how, exactly, can we accomplish this in our daily lives?

Here is the 5-step process that we have found to be most effective. We use the acronym, S.M.A.R.T., to make these steps memorable.

Set Your Intentions

Maximize Your Mindfulness

Activate Your Strengths

Reconcile Gaps

Take Action

1. Set Your Intentions

Above all, answering The Central Question requires a high desire to be valuegenic. When you honestly ask yourself The Central Question, it automatically creates a mental shift. It begins the process of exploring what choices you have and potential actions you could take that could result in creating greater net value. It shifts you out of any self-centric mindset and into a valuegenic mindset. It empowers and engages your conscious mind so that you are not simply operating in the habitual, reactive mode of your auto-conscience. Remember, The Central Question, like the clutch in an automobile, tends to disengage your low VQs from running your thoughts.

You may find it very helpful, once you have asked yourself The Central Question, to make note of whatever options, choices, or considerations immediately come to mind. Whatever comes up at this point may have significant intuitive value and is probably worthy of further exploration in the steps that follow.

2. Maximize Your Mindfulness

The next step is to become highly observant of your thoughts and emotions. Learn to recognize the warning signs that you are operating from auto-conscience and/or a low-VQ perspective. The most obvious signs are our emotional reactions to stimuli (things that happen, things other people do or say, etc.). Other signs include stress, over-excitement, procrastination, rationalization, conflict, confusion, and indecision.

When you are engaged in activities that involve other people, you will want to pay close attention to them. Observe their actions and emotions. Listen to what they are saying. "Tune" into them using your "in-tune-ition" and empathy.

3. Activate Your Strengths

Use your Centering Questions to power shift your mental gears so that your focus and attention is coming from the high-VQ perspective (strength) that seems most relevant to the situation. Asking yourself Centering Questions tends to cause you to relax and to open your mind to possibilities and insights. By opening up you are better able to connect new information with other information stored in your memory so you can more effectively analyze all the available information, both rationally and intuitively. Your desire to find answers to a Centering Question will lead you to discovering the best answer you can.

In our coaching and self-study programs, clients are given Centering Questions for *all* of their primary strengths. Knowing all your Centering Questions is like putting this whole process on steroids and gives you more options and greater flexibility .

However, the process still works, even if all you have are the Centering Questions from your free assessment report. You can even use The Central Question as a "catch-all" Centering Question to help you shift into your higher-conscience.

From our higher-conscience, we all have capacities far beyond our limited and limiting habitual ways. The only reason we may not exercise this capacity is that we allow our low VQs to interfere. The more we strengthen our true strengths, the less susceptible we become to that interference.

4. Reconcile Gaps

Look for any gaps in perception, knowledge, understanding, or priorities. Remember, your high VQs will help you see these gaps as opportunities to create value rather than as threats (as low VQs would). Your Centering Questions will help you explore whatever you need to explore in order to reconcile or accept any gaps, until they are no longer a limit to potential value generation.

It's also important to keep the Hierarchy of Value (Intrinsic > Extrinsic > Systemic) in mind. This will help you make better, more accurate value judgments and help mitigate any interference from low VQs that might cause you to make a value misjudgment.

Be sure to explore whatever came to mind when you first asked yourself The Central Question. How often have you "known" what you "should do," then allowed your mind (your low VQs) to rationalize and justify all the reasons why not to do it. This time, let your strengths do the work. Consider your choices and actions from the perspective of the value they might create, rather than what they might cost.

From this highly conscious and curious mindset, centered in your strengths, and focused on value creation, you are much more likely to reconcile any relevant gaps. You will gain knowledge, insight, and understanding of your options and be more likely put/keep things in their proper axiological place. In short, you'll be using all of your best thinking to seek and find a good answer The Central Question.

5. Take Action

Having a good answer to The Central Question is meaningless if you don't actually take the action. After all, the whole point is to decide what action has the potential to create the greatest net value. Therefore, the final step is to take the action and create the value.

With practice, this process will become more and more natural because all you are doing is tapping into that part of your thinking that is already naturally SMART. Sometimes, the entire process may take no more than a few seconds, especially when the gaps are few and "the answer" is obvious. Other times, however, it may take a bit more time and effort, particularly when the gaps are significant, the stakes are high, the interference from your low VQs is strong, or you have multiple options to consider.

Making real and lasting positive change in our habits of mind takes repetitive, effective practice. The more you practice, the easier it gets and the less "deliberate" you need to be.

> "There is nothing noble about being superior to some other person. The true nobility is in being superior to your previous self."
>
> ~ Hindustani Proverb

• • •

MAGIC Moments and Opportunities

> You have the power to deliberately create MAGIC in your life—if you look for the opportunities and apply SMART principles.

> "Logic only gives man what he needs...Magic gives him what he wants."
>
> ~ Tom Robbins

When you rise above your auto-conscience and engage your true strengths, seemingly magical things begin to happen. Most amazing is how often, when you apply the SMART process, you will create results that seem almost "MAGICal."

MAGIC is an acronym we use for: Moments of Awareness that Generate Insight and Choice. Why MAGIC? Because they are moments of opportunity to make weaknesses vanish and wisdom emerge "out of thin air." You can transform challenge into opportunity, procrastination into action, division into partnership, conflict into connection, and anger into awareness. You can pull a metaphorical "rabbit out of a hat," producing unexpected results in your life. In these moments, you can be a master magician, a wizard of wonderment and curiosity, an alchemist of awareness, a sage of strengths, and a virtuoso of valuegenic living. In these moments, you can set a process in motion that creates seemingly magical results and sends ripples of value far beyond the immediate benefits.

Of course, there is actually nothing magical about MAGIC moments, other than our experience of being amazed by the results. There is no sleight of hand, deception, or misdirection involved. MAGIC is simply the result of natural principles at work. Yet, what is life but a string of moments? What is success but making a series of more SMART choices and actions than bad ones?

MAGIC is born out of a willful desire to look for opportunities to create greater value through deliberate SMART practice. Through self-awareness, you observe the warning signs that a low-VQ "mental program" is either in control or trying to take over. Through awareness and sensitivity to other people and situations you gain insight and perspective. By reconciling gaps, you gain even more insight, knowledge and wisdom.

Let me illustrate the power of SMART MAGIC with a story of my own . . .

Headline: Man Thwarts Hijacking With SMART MAGIC

It's Saturday night. My wife Pam, Hannah our daughter, and I have plans to go see a close friend play music at a local restaurant. We needed to leave by 8:00 PM to be there on time and find good seats. I was ready at 7:30 and, being an amateur musician myself, thought I would use the extra time to start writing a song for an upcoming coaching conference. The song was about "choosing the good" and it just flowed right out of me: the lyrics, the melody, the music—everything. It was one of those experiences when it felt like something or someone else inside me wrote it. I was excited and couldn't wait to share it with Pam and Hannah.

At about 8:10, they finally came downstairs and announced, with bubbly anticipation of a fun night together, that they were ready to go. I said, "Ok, but let me play you this song that I just wrote," and I started to strum the guitar. "Pete, we don't have time," replied Pam. "Can't we just go?" Hannah added, "We're already late."

"But it will only take a few minutes," I protested. "What's the big deal? It's a really good song about making good choices in pivotal moments of life."

Pam's body language shifted; she stiffened, ready to put her foot down. "Pete, your song can wait. We need to leave now!"

I was flabbergasted. Music was a huge part of our life. It was partly my music playing that initially attracted her to me. I imagined playing this song at the conference and getting a glorious standing ovation. She had encouraged me to write more music, and now that I had, she didn't want to hear it!

"Wow, do I feel devalued," I declared. "Why do we always have to follow your agenda? This is really important to me. I thought you would be excited, and instead you just ripped into me." '*Go by yourself then,*' I thought to myself; but didn't say, as I turned away.

"Are you coming or not?" Pam asked, with a last-chance-or-we're-leaving tone to her voice.

"OK, fine! Boy, you can be so systemic!" I complained as I set down the guitar, none too gently. We went to the car. I was brooding, obviously upset with everyone, and I didn't know (or even care) if they were upset with me. All I knew was that I was hurt, felt disvalued, and wasn't about to act happy and talkative on the ride to the restaurant. I lost that battle; but I was going to win the war!

Let's pause the story and look at what's really going on here. Was I valuing Pam, my wife, or Hannah, my daughter, as the unique and irreplaceable human beings they are and whom I love as much as life itself (intrinsic)? No. Was I being sensitive to what they wanted to do and the fun evening they were looking forward to having (extrinsic)? No. Was I keeping our agreement to get to the restaurant on time (systemic)? No. Clearly, there were some unreconciled gaps and I was engulfed in a full-blown amygdala hijack. My auto-conscious habits let my amygdala hijack my thoughts, emotions, actions, and reactions. Was I being SMART? No, "I" was out of control. I was being a Disvaluing, Unforgiving, Me-centered, Bullhead (DUMB).

Now, back to the story . . . five minutes later, it hit me. As I replayed the scene in my head, with every intention of justifying why I should be upset, I got what seemed like an "instant message" in my mind—'*you've been hijacked*'—and I suddenly realized what had happened. But, I still had some nasty neuropeptides flowing through my system, so my next automatic thought was no more valuegenic than the hijack itself. I found myself going deeper into the abyss by getting angry *at myself* for allowing it to happen, and at Pam and Hannah for "making" it happen.

Thanks to the "instant message" though, I was forewarned and fore-rearmed. Maintaining a sufficient level of mindfulness, I was quickly able to recognize that I had violated the Hierarchy of Value—I had let old habits put the systemic ahead of the intrinsic. I quickly asked myself The Central Question and immediately calmed down. This enabled me to ask myself a Centering Question related to a high-VQ perspective (one pertaining to my ability to forgive myself and learn from my mistakes). It was at that moment that the irony of the situation struck me square in the funny bone and I burst out laughing.

Now, you can imagine what must have been going on for Pam and Hannah. Here I had been angry, upset, and giving them the silent treatment, then all of a sudden I'm laughing. Clearly, I had gone off the deep end.

Pam asked what I was laughing at and I told her: "I'm laughing at myself and the crazy way my auto-conscious mind can take over so quickly, despite all my "work" on myself. I had just written this great song about choosing the good and about being value-centered. Then, when you didn't want to take the time to hear it, I immediately did the exact opposite of what the song itself was about! I made you wrong for being so systemic, while I was being even more systemic myself. Then I started to beat myself up over it, which just made it worse."

"You know," Pam said, "that's not really all that funny." "No, it's not," I agreed. "It was self-centered, arrogant, and not very nice. I guess I still have some work to do."

"So do I," she admitted, as she put a loving, comforting hand on mine. "I think I could have handled that a lot better too."

What might have happened if I had asked if it was okay to play the song, rather than insisting? What might have happened if I had said, "Okay, it can wait."? What if I had been more valuegenic at the outset?

What might have happened if Pam had said, "You wrote a song just now? Tell me what it's about." Or even, "Wow, honey, that's amazing. I'd love to hear it. How about if you play it for me as soon as we get home tonight? We'd really like to get to the restaurant before the good seats fill up."

There are many fascinating axiological aspects to this story. What Pam and Hannah said to me was not really a devaluation of me (intrinsic), but I took it that way (systemic). I clearly had my agenda and a desire to impress them with my brilliance (extrinsic). I had a systemic expectation that they would want to hear the song. Pam and Hannah had their agendas and expectations (systemic), along with lots of excitement about the fun evening we would all have together (intrinsic).

The perspectives we all adopted in that moment were all from low VQs and in complete violation of axiogenic principles. At the time, my systemic perspective was the lowest of all my VQs, and it showed. My auto-conscience took over and, for a short while, I was blind to anyone's intrinsic value. I was hurt and I made Pam wrong for it! I had placed the systemic above the intrinsic. The gaps had become abyss-like pits of emotional upheaval.

Where's the MAGIC?

Thankfully, I was able to turn my hijack into a MAGIC opportunity. Within seconds of adopting a more valuegenic mindfulness the upset and anger began to vanish. I activated my higher VQs and immediately began to see the gaps and to perceive completely new possibilities from my new perspective.

I have little doubt that Pam would have gotten past the upset eventually. However, it may have put quite a damper on the evening. Instead, by deliberately choosing to be value-centered, we quickly re-established our loving partnership and we all had a glorious evening together. It truly was one of those MAGICal moments—**M**oments of **A**wareness that **G**enerate **I**nsight and **C**hoice.

· · ·

You Can Create MAGIC Now

You already have the power to create MAGIC. With the right tools and a little SMART practice, you'll be amazed at what you can achieve.

"Joy comes from using your potential."

~ Will Schultz

Based on our experience with thousands of assessments, we estimate that well over 80% of the population has a pattern in their value structure that could easily have them react to "rejection" in much the same way as I did at first. However, not everyone knows how to make the SMART shift. The only difference between them and me is that I have had the benefit of working extensively with these principles over a number of years. Still, I'm a very long way from "perfect."

How many families and partnerships do you know have fallen apart because they let their low VQs run the show and the frustration, pain, and anger grew until it festered like a cancer.

How many people keep their stress and anxiety bottled up inside and suffer (along with their loved ones) from devastating, stress-induced dis-eases as a result? How much value, creativity, productivity, communication, and love is lost because people hold back out of fear, distrust, self-protection, or even revenge? Dr. Hartman measured it at 40%![37]

Even though 80% of the population may be at risk for such challenges, 80% also have sufficient high VQs to make better choices; to choose more valuegenic perspectives, to be more accountable and responsible, and to turn challenging moments into opportunities to create MAGIC. They often don't make these choices simply because they don't know they can, and/or they don't know how.

From this day forth, you don't have to be one of them. You now have the basic knowledge and tools you need to start being SMART about how you approach your life/work. So long as you use these principles to keep answering The Central Question to the best of your ever-improving ability, you'll be engaged in the Process of Continuous Value Generation and bringing ever-increasing value to life.

The next chapter offers a deeper exploration of what a valuegenic organization looks like. We will also explore some of the issues involved in developing such an organization and what the real-world, practical benefits can be.

• • •

> "The potential of the average person is like a huge ocean unsailed, a new continent unexplored, a world of possibilities waiting to be released and channeled toward some great good."
>
> ~ Brian Tracy

---

[37] (R. S. Hartman 1963)

The Valuegenic
Organization

"If you're not interested in leaving a larger legacy than wealth or
social status, you're in business for the wrong reasons."

~ *Glenn Llopis*

"If human beings are perceived as potentials rather than problems,
as possessing strengths instead of weaknesses, as unlimited rather than
dull and unresponsive, then they thrive and grow to their capabilities."

~ *Barbara Bush*

The Value of Being a Valuegenic Organization

Valuegenic organizations make more money, attract and keep better employees, and make a bigger difference in the world.

"Survival and profit are fine, but if you don't have values or 'higher purpose' at the heart of your business, you may be losing out in the battle for the hearts and minds of customers, suppliers and employees."

~ Rick Spence[38]

What leader of an organization is not interested in increasing the organization's performance? The Natural Laws of Value and the related axiogenic principles are universal. Therefore, they apply just as much to organizations with thousands of people as they do to individuals. A valuegenic organization, whether you call it that or not:

- Exudes value-centeredness in its culture: value-centeredness is a primary organizational Value;
- Actually recognizes and believes that people are the organization's most precious asset;
- Encourages people's innate valuegenic desire to find their own answers to The Central Question;
- Embeds the Process of Continuous Value Generation in everything it does;
- Adheres to the Hierarchy of Value in its structure, policies, and procedures, and clearly promotes valuegenic principles as a standard of leadership, decision-making, personal interaction, and performance;
- Proactively coaches, mentors, teaches, and trains all employees, regardless of title or position, in the principles of value generation; and
- Holds people accountable for, rewards, and celebrates valuegenic thinking and leadership.

---

[38] Toronto-based small business strategist and entrepreneurship columnist for the National Post.

An organization is fundamentally a collective of people. Any organization can become valuegenic by following the very same essential principles that individuals would follow. The context may change, but the process is the same.

Let's look at the implications of the core principles of Axiogenics from an organizational perspective:

1. **"Value drives success in all endeavors."**
    An organization exists to create value for its stakeholders by adding value to society. The more value an organization creates, the greater its success. To maximize success, every decision and action people make must be in an effort to fulfill that purpose.

2. **"Your mind-brain is already value-driven."**
    The choices and actions of every person who has a stake in your organization are driven by their perceptions of value—both the opportunities they have to create value and the value they will receive in return. To maximize success, you need to manage the value equation and optimize VQ.

3. **"There is a universal Hierarchy of Value (HOV)"**
    The HOV reveals the universal framework for valuegenic decision-making and policy-making. When we try to violate it, we create a loss of value. Understanding the HOV allows us to utilize the Process of Continuous Value Generation to maximize organizational success.

4. **"Accurately answering The Central Question is the key to maximizing your success."**
    The most successful companies in the world recognize that the greatest threat to success is anything that limits people's potential to generate value through their ideas, choices, and actions. The spirit of The Central Question permeates their culture at every level.

The benefits of becoming a more valuegenic organization are many and extend from the employment line to the bottom line. Let's take a look at the evidence.

The Evidence

Since 1980, Great Place to Work Institute, Inc. (GPWI) has re-searched the qualities and behaviors that create great workplaces. GPWI ranks companies based on extensive surveys and interviews of employees from nominated companies. After nearly 30 years, they have a good handle on the factors that make a "great place to work" and how those factors translate into success. We suggest that GPWI's data reinforces the value of becoming a valuegenic organization.

Reason #1:

According to the GPWI[39], what puts companies on the list of *Best Companies to Work For®* is that employees have a positive view of their leaders' credibility, they feel respected by management, and the company's policies and practices are viewed as being fair and appropriate.

The GPWI also contends, "Employees also place significant value on the pride they feel in the work they do, the reputation of their companies and of the tremendous camaraderie they experience among their co-workers." Notice that virtually all of the attributes that GPWI lists as being most important, are about how people feel:

- Credibility of Leaders—Can they be trusted?
- Respect of Employees—Do they honor and trust me?
- Fairness—Do they treat me fairly and without prejudice?
- Pride—Is there an intrinsic value of work?

These attributes have little or nothing to do with profits, pay scales, or the company size or location. We contend that what makes the difference, though they may not realize it, is that their culture is more

---

[39] http://www.greatplacetowork.com, 9/5/2009

closely aligned with the Hierarchy of Value. Great companies are value-centered; their center of focus is on improving the quality of life for people (intrinsic value), including their owners, employees, customers, and community.

So, as we have seen, a valuegenic organization can be a great place to work, but does that equate to higher productivity and profitability? Yes, it does.

Reason #2

After more than 100 years of research, GPWI confirms that the "Best Companies":

- Receive more qualified job applications for open positions
- Experience a lower level of turnover
- Are less negatively impacted by employee stress
- Enjoy higher levels of customer satisfaction and loyalty
- Foster greater innovation, creativity, and risk taking
- Benefit from higher productivity and profitability[40]

If you look at the top 100 list of the *Best Companies to Work For®* as listed by *Fortune* Magazine from 1998 to 2008 (which includes the dot-com stock boom), you'll discover that the best companies delivered an average return to investors of 6.80% while the S&P 500 returned an average of just 1.04%. That's a 650% higher return for "Best" companies:[41] a tremendous pay off for simply following the natural law!

Reason #3

GPWI research affirms what Dr. Hartman discovered nearly 20 years earlier. Dr. Hartman demonstrated that when people in an organization are valued intrinsically first (as people) and extrinsically second (as worker-producers)—they will unleash an average of 40% more

---

[40] (Great Place to Work Institute - Results n.d.)
[41] (Great Place to Work Institute - Financial Results n.d.)

cooperation and productivity.[42] Said another way, in the absence of a culture that celebrates and "lives" axiogenic principles, employees will withhold an average of 40% of their potential. Quite simply, they will preserve the best of their talent, creativity, and energy for something or someone who will value them more.

If you and/or your organization are not performing at the level you would like, it's going to require some change.

· · ·

Organizational Culture and Change

The overall culture of any organization is a direct reflection of the composite value structure (VQ) of its people. Change the people's value structures, change the culture.

> "Change is hard because people overestimate the value of what they have - and underestimate the value of what they may gain by giving that up."
>
> ~ James Belasco and Ralph Stayer

What's the point of having a "core values statement" if the culture, policies, and management style of the organization are not aligned with the Values? Not much, if any. When a company's stated "Values" become more like the company joke, it can actually create skepticism, cynicism, disloyalty, diminished performance, and cultural toxicity.

When organizational leadership actively works to nurture and develop a valuegenic culture, the organization's core vision, mission, and value statements take on a new energy. Not only do they become statements of what the company stands for, they become statements that employees *make a stand for* because the statements also represent their own personal aspirations.

---

[42] (R. S. Hartman 1963)

Organizations do not have value structures; they have a culture. An organization's culture is a composite of the individual value structures (VQ profiles) of its people molded by a number of factors into an often rather fuzzy shape. These molding factors include:

- The power of formal and informal authority figures
- The degree of similarities and dissimilarities in the value structures among the individuals
- The clarity and consistency of the mission
- Organizational traditions, rituals, and ceremonies
- The quality of relationships between people
- The handling of successes and failures at every level
- Gaps between expectations and reality

Individual divisions and departments may have their own distinct cultures. Within each division or department, the various teams and crews can also have their own unique culture.

Organizations and cultures are collections of unique individuals and real change has to occur at the individual, personal level. The bad news is that culture is extremely difficult to change through broad behavioral approaches, motivational events, or systemic policy changes.

The good news is that people are driven by their VQ and most people already have a several high VQs that could align with or support changes that are value-driven. Essentially, you don't need to fix people to improve the culture, you just need to liberate their highest VQs. While that's easily said, in reality it takes leadership, the right tools, and the willingness to invest the necessary effort and resources.

The best news is that the desire to create greater value is universal. Conversations about creating greater value open up people's minds and engage their high VQs. They help people to see change as a positive opportunity rather than a threat. They motivate and inspire people to be part of something greater than the status quo. They paint pictures of possibilities for a future in which people naturally want to invest their best efforts. Such conversations are contagious and create positive ripple effects throughout the culture.

> "Most important, leaders can conceive and articulate goals that lift people out of their petty preoccupations and unite them in pursuit of objectives worthy of their best efforts."
>
> ~ John Gardner

Ultimately, if you want to change an entire culture, you have to work to bring the most influential leaders into alignment with the new direction. If these people don't align with the vision, one of two things has to happen: change the vision or change the people.

When leaders are committed to creating a valuegenic organizational culture, they must come to grips with the possibility that not everyone will follow along. Some people, including some leaders and managers, may be too gripped by either fear or arrogance (or both) to engage in the process. Some people will react with resistance, sabotaging behaviors, refusal to participate, or even view themselves as above the process and not needing to engage. Some people will leave. When people leave, it makes room for new people who want to be part of the new culture, and that can be a good thing.

To understand how to prevent the saboteurs from undermining change initiatives, it's important to understand something about the nature of change resistance from an axiogenic perspective.

VQ Can Drive Both Change and Resistance

Organizational change usually creates a situation in which people must deal with things unknown: like how well something will work or how it will impact their future. They may perceive trouble ahead, think that they will lose something they value, or will have to do more work. The list could go on and on, but underneath the resistance to change will be a perception that the change does not add value or could potentially take value away. A resistance to change that is motivated by a self-centric interest (low-VQ perspective) carries a high risk of resentment, sabotage, and retaliation.

However, resistance to change can be a good thing when it is coming from a high-VQ perspective. This "resistance" may actually be intuitive wisdom that there are potential problems with the proposed change. This may be an opportunity to collaborate in designing changes that can create even greater net value than the original idea.

Now, consider the following:

> *A person's capacity to __create__ value is limited by their capacity to __conceive and perceive__ value (by their VQ).*

A person's value perceptions and judgments are driven by the VQ of the perspective from which they view the issue. The lower their VQ, the less accurate their judgments may be. Because people's efforts and actions are value-driven, if they are being self-centric, they are likely to give a level of effort only equal to the value they perceive they will get.

This dynamic can cut both ways. On one hand, if they underestimate the value they will get for their efforts (lower expectations), or over-estimate the personal cost of their efforts, they are likely to give less effort (under-performance). On the other hand, if they overestimate the value they will get for their efforts (higher expectations), or under-estimate the personal cost of their efforts, they may work harder for a time, but may then become resentful if they don't get the rewards, recognition, or even the satisfaction they expect.

Any low VQ has the potential of lowering the total (net) value that a person can conceive and perceive in any given moment. To minimize this risk, you want to increase their ability to use more of their high-VQ strengths and not let their low VQs get in the way.

If you try to force someone to change without helping them see the net positive value of the change *for themselves*, they will naturally resent and resist the change. They may change for a while (e.g., out of a fear of consequences), but there will likely come a time when they will either revert back to old behaviors, compensate in some way (make you pay for it), or new, unwanted behaviors may inadvertently surface. These may include rebellion, covert sabotage, decreased morale, lower performance in some other area of responsibility, problems at home, stress-induced self-destructive behaviors, and other negative consequences.

An axiogenic approach not only reduces resistance, it also provides a powerful means to deal with those individuals that may resist change—people we might call "roadblockers."

> "Progress is impossible without change and those who cannot change their minds cannot change anything."
>
> ~ George Bernard Shaw

Handling the Roadblockers

In working with organizations and teams, there are four types of people to watch out for. Keep in mind, that while we may seem to be labeling people in this discussion, we are using the labels only to indicate *where* a person is, not *who* he is. We want to emphasize that, though people may start out in one of these mindsets, it is quite rare that they remain there when axiogenic principles are applied. On those rare occasions when they are unable to make the shift, one of two things happens: they leave the organization (by choice or otherwise) or they attempt to sabotage the process!

The Fixer

This is someone who thinks everyone else is the problem. They believe they are already masterful at answering The Central Question. They may attempt to take on a leadership role in the transformation process but not see any need to take on their own "stuff." Alternatively, a Fixer may prefer to stay on the sidelines "waiting" for everyone else to "catch up" with them.

Appeal to the Fixers to engage in the process of change so they can help drive it. If they have a more intimate understanding of axiogenic principles, they will be in a better position to contribute to other people's growth process. Once they do get involved, invariably they begin to see things about themselves they had not seen before and they will become more engaged as participants. Fixers can sometimes become the greatest advocates of change initiatives since they often see opportunities for shifts in their own lives. However, they can also become somewhat arrogant advocates. Most often, within a valuegenic organization, even this changes naturally with time and good coaching.

The Ostrich

An Ostrich is someone who refuses to acknowledge that there is any need or room for improvement. Usually, it's caused by a value structure that overvalues the status quo or is simply uncomfortable with change. They may have some fear about what will happen to them if other people "do better" in the change process. They may have a view of themselves that they are who they are and that they can't change or grow. Ostriches are relatively easy to enroll once they begin to see the possibilities and feel safe as valued participants in the process.

The Agnostic

The Agnostic is someone who thinks the entire concept of being valuegenic (and the idea that there is a universal Hierarchy of Value) is little more than touchy-feely snake oil. Agnostics often wind up either changing their minds as they see things change around them or they eventually leave the organization. If they don't get on board quickly, though, they may actively start working covertly, or even overtly, against the process. If there is a "devout agnostic" in a leadership or management role, and they have the power to railroad the process, it is generally best to nip the problem in the bud and help them find a new organization to call home. However, when an Agnostic does make the transition and becomes a "believer," the pendulum can sometimes swing so far the other way that they become either a Fixer or a Manipulator. With good coaching and mentoring, this will level out in time. It's just part of the process.

The Manipulator

The Manipulator is someone who sees change as an opportunity to gain power, greater control, or otherwise advance their own self-centric agenda. Like Agnostics, Manipulators can cause serious problems if they are in management or leadership roles. They will attempt to use (abuse or misuse) axiogenic principles as a weapon for their own advantage. Some do it consciously and intentionally while others may be unaware they are doing it (Manipulator-Fixer). In a valuegenic organization, manipulation doesn't usually work for very long. As a result, Manipulators tend to embrace the process very early on because they see an advantage in doing so. However, when manipulation stops working, they may start to complain that the program "doesn't work." At that point, under the care and guidance of a gifted coach, Manipulators often go through a powerful and positive transformation.

• • •

Developing a Valuegenic Organization

Creating a valuegenic organization is easier than you may think. It's a natural process driven by natural law.

"We can reach our potential, but to do so, we must reach within ourselves. We must summon the strength, the will, and the faith to move forward - to be bold - to invest in our future."

~ John Hoeven

Perhaps the greatest barrier to organizational transformation is the common belief that people can't change and that investing in "soft skills" development is a waste of time and money. Frankly, we don't blame leaders for having this attitude since many of the more common approaches to training and development have failed to produce significant returns on investment. In other words, they often don't work very well. They don't work because they don't go deep enough to create changes at the source of motivation and address the real challenge—changing people's fundamental value structures and thought processes.

Let's face it though, if you walk into the office next week with this book in hand and expect everyone to jump on board with great enthusiasm, you'll probably be disappointed. Remember, people are hesitant to make changes, they don't like to be "fixed," and they can be very skeptical of anything "new."

So what can you do?

Start Where You Are Now

Paraphrasing Gandhi, the best way to let others see that change is possible, is to 'become the change you want to see.' So the first step is to take on the process of becoming more valuegenic in your own life and work. Lead by example. Demonstrate the difference in yourself. At the very least, you gain the personal rewards of improved quality of life.

Regardless of your current position or level of authority, you are a leader. Leadership is not about *controlling* people, it's about influencing them in positive, value-generating ways. The origin of the verb "to lead" comes from the Old English word, *lædan*, and means "cause to go with, to travel."[43] To lead means to cause people to go, to move, to change positions. Is there any doubt that you influence other people in every interaction, directly or indirectly? Is there any doubt that you have influenced and been influenced by your interactions with others? You are always leading, influencing, and causing change. Your choices and actions have a ripple effect. What ripples are you sending out? The question is, are you leading people toward *greater* value or *less* value?

You have influence on everyone around you. No matter what your job title is, you ARE a leader. At the very least, you are the leader of YOU and your thoughts. In the previous chapter, you learned how to manage those 36 VQ perspectives to maximize your own performance. Creating a valuegenic organization starts with you becoming the leader of you. Take it on!

---

[43] http://dictionary.reference.com/browse/lead, 9/18/2009

"I'm starting with the man in the mirror
I'm asking him to change his ways
and no message could have been any clearer
if you wanna make the world a better place
take a look at yourself, and then make a change."

~ *Michael Jackson, from Man in the Mirror*

Create a Core Group

Having done the work on yourself and in your own life/work, you'll have the credibility and influence to become a change agent in your organization. The next step is to enroll others with influence in the organization to engage in the process for their *personal* benefit. Start having conversations about how *your* life has changed and the possibilities for *their* life. The goal is to create a core group of influential people who are experiencing (and demonstrating through example) the benefits of being valuegenic in their own lives.

Once you have a core group of advocate-leaders engaged in the process on a *personal* level, it's time to work together to create a greater vision for the future of the organization and begin to advocate that vision to others.

Create a SMART Leadership Culture

In a SMART leadership culture, every employee feels genuinely valued. They know they have influence on the future of the organization and an important contribution to make. From top to bottom, people look to find the best possible answers to The Central Question and they don't need to be afraid to voice their ideas. Dr. Hartman proved that people will give, on average, 40% more of themselves when they feel valued as human beings first and employees or co-workers second.

You can start by mentoring other managers and leaders. Help them elicit the best in people's VQs. Teach them The Central Question and the principles of SMART thinking. By doing nothing more than unleashing *existing* high-VQ potential, you will increase performance—the kind of performance great organizations exhibit.

When people start to operate out of their high VQs, instead of their low VQs, they think *and feel* better. This alters the entire process of change, growth, and cultural transformation. For example, what would be more effective: establishing new policies and procedures when people are operating from low VQs that resist change, or enrolling people in the possibilities of change when they are coming from high-VQ perspectives? When a preponderance of people in a culture are thinking valuegenically, both cultural transformation and continuous value creation are the natural outcomes.

· · ·

Increasing Your Training ROI

> Make sure your people are using their highest VQs before you spend time and money on other training and development.

How does being valuegenic impact other kinds of training and development, such as technical education, diversity, or team-building? Hopefully, it's become obvious that getting people to think better, *before* you spend money on other kinds of training just makes good sense. When people participate in "how-to" training and development from a high-VQ perspective, they have a genuine desire to learn how to create greater value. Therefore, they naturally learn and integrate the training better and faster.

In fact, you may need to spend a lot *less* money on soft-skills training and development than ever before. When people become more valuegenic, their "people skills" naturally improve. They become self-invested as life-long students in the art of creating value.

Once you've planted the seeds of a valuegenic culture, "soft-skills" training can become more informal and mentor-driven. At least some of the money spent on formal "soft-skills" training and development can then be put to better use.

· · ·

Don't Guess, Assess!

If you want to know the true health of your organization's culture and the stress points that may be "making it sick," assess the VQ profiles of your people and look at the composite results. Since value structures drive the process of all human choice, action, and reaction, value structures also drive the performance of an organization's people and, therefore, the organization itself.

VQ Profiling is a unique and powerful form of SWOT (Strengths, Weaknesses, Opportunities and Threats) analysis. It identifies an organization's strengths, weaknesses, opportunities for development, and threats to success that are present in both the composite and individual VQ profiles of its people. A special composite analysis report is available to corporate clients.

VQ Profiling also enables us to "benchmark" the critical VQ factors that differentiate between high and low performers in specific roles within an individual organization. By identifying these factors, leaders and managers can make better hiring, promotion, and training decisions to optimize their workforce.

• • •

CHAPTER
8

More Possibilities

"The difference between what we do and what we are capable of doing would suffice to solve most of the world's problems."

~ Mahatma Gandhi

What follows is a selection of essays that present additional possibilities for how The Central Question can bring value to the world. Our hope is that you will find these essays informative, useful and perhaps even inspiring.

The Valuegenic Salesperson

Stop "selling" and you'll probably sell more!

The word "sell" comes from an old English word, *sellan*, which literally means "to give." Selling is about *giving* value, not getting the order. A valuegenic salesperson looks at a prospect and sees a human being, not dollar signs. They explore the prospect's needs, wants, desires, and concerns long before attempting to get them to buy anything. They engage in "gain-gain negotiation" and look for ways to add real value— *from the prospect's perspective.*

Sales, like many interactions, often involves negotiations. Each party has something they want out of the process. A valuegenic approach to negotiation can be used to create a partnership in which each participant fully listens, hears, honors, and considers the other person's desires, expectations, concerns, limits, and perceptions.

In negotiation, as in many aspects of life, the whole is generally greater than the parts. As the old adage goes, "Two heads are better than one." A healthy negotiation is one in which both parties bring out the best thinking in the other. All limits and gaps are acknowledged or reconciled and neither party "dominates" the other. The goal is not to "win," but to optimize value for both parties: a gain-gain outcome.

The Hierarchy of Value provides a framework for approaching and completing a gain-gain negotiation (intrinsic > extrinsic > systemic). This approach, if well and honestly executed, will create a solution that optimizes value for both parties *every time*. It's very simple (but, not always easy). You need to be able to use your strengths (high VQs) and keep both The Central Question and the Process of Continuous Value Generation in mind.

When you give up a self/sell-centric approach and instead seek to serve and create gain-gain value, you will have more success.

• • •

The Valuegenic Early-Stage Investor

> Axiogenics could very well be a game-changer for Angels, VCs, and small Private Equity investors; providing a powerful new way to measure and develop people's talent for success.

Businesses don't succeed or fail; people do. Depending on who you talk to, statistically somewhere between 70% and 90% of the companies in which VCs or Angels invest, fail to produce a meaningful return on investment or even the invested principle.

The "game" of investing is about finding businesses that (a) have the potential to increase substantially in value, (b) need capital (and perhaps other resources and connections) to succeed, (c) the investor can work with to add value, and (d) are within the investor's risk tolerance.

"It is said that a venture capitalist spends more time bemoaning failures than celebrating wins," says Michael Gurau, general partner at Clear Venture Partners. "In part, I suspect, that is because there are statistically more of the former than the latter. Good early-stage VCs 'bat .333,' with the few wins making up for the many losses."[44]

Historically, investors target an aggregate internal rate of return (IRR) of around 20%. Under the prevailing paradigm, the strategy for accomplishing this is to balance successes with failures, and exit strategies with ROIs. Essentially, it's been a numbers game.

Using a baseball analogy, the approach most investors take is to find home run hitters. If they don't think they have a home run hitter, they will not invest. Of course, they also know that only a handful will actually hit a home run, while the vast majority will strike out. This is why they need the home runs and why they demand an exit strategy that can give them a 10x ROI. Using simple math, if two out of ten hit a home run (at least 10x ROI), and the rest return nothing, the result is an average ROI of 20%. We think there is a better approach that can return a much higher ROI.

---

[44] (Gurau, Gurau, Failure comes with the venture capitalist's job, 2010 2010)

The real cause of failure is often not the product or market. The real problem is that too many of the management teams in which direct investors invest, don't seem to have what it takes to get a base-hit, let alone a home run, and neither the investor nor the entrepreneur realizes it until it's too late.

Of course, investors do their best to investigate the management team by doing background checks, looking at their history, and getting a "feel" for the people. But, under the prevailing business model, investors would never invest in an opportunity if they didn't believe that the management team had the potential to hit a grand-slam home run. However, still only a small percentage of investments actually become winners.

The great pity in all this is that many fabulous business ideas come from creative entrepreneurs with little or no track record. Unfortunately, they have no history to support the level of comfort investors need. As a result, many great ideas and potentially lucrative opportunities never get the help *they* need.

A Valuegenic Paradigm for Investing

For the first time in history, we have a fast, reliable, objective, and cost-effective way to determine if an entrepreneur or management team has or can develop the leadership and management skills required for success. For early and middle-stage business investors, VQ profiling can be a game-changer.

Profiling a management team's VQ can give you a level of foresight that goes far beyond what most due diligence can provide. You can identify, in advance, the issues that usually are discovered only in hindsight—when an investment is nearly lost, a business is floundering, a lawsuit is filed, a poor hiring decision is made, or even a marriage is on the rocks. How important is this? According to Gurau, "Although a softer skill set, and therefore more challenging to research, emotional intelligence is perhaps the most important indicator of founder/CEO success in a company."[45] Of course, as we pointed out earlier in this book, VQ is what determines EQ, thus making VQ even more important than EQ.

Obviously, many variables can and will influence the success of any endeavor. Assessing VQ is not a replacement for good old-fashioned due diligence. However, here are just a few things we can measure with extraordinary accuracy:

- Integrity
- Self-confidence
- Ability to focus
- Ability to prioritize
- Ability to delegate
- Ability to give clear direction
- Capacity to listen to ideas
- Respect for authority
- Leadership qualities
- Ability to understand and embrace detail and complexity
- Ability to set realistic goals and expectations
- Ability to operate effectively under stress and chaos
- Ability to assess other people
- Prejudice and tolerance
- Ability to make good use of resources
- Creativity
- Systematic thinking

- Empathy
- Compassion
- Persistence
- Ability to establish and/or follow rules, order and structure
- Loyalty
- Coachability
- Passion
- Management qualities
- Self-discipline
- Pragmatism
- Ability to establish and maintain order and structure
- Perfectionism
- Tendencies to procrastinate
- Argumentativeness
- Motivating factors
- Need to have things their way
- Openness to ideas
- Change resistance/insistence
- Risk aversion/tolerance

---

[45] (Gurau, Entrepreneur, Coach Thyself 2006)

Using this kind of "crystal ball" to look into the minds of potential investees gives investors an edge and allows them to make better investment decisions.

And that's just the beginning! Assessing the VQ of a management team and their key employees allows investors to:

- Find out if the leader and/or team has the fundamental talent, fortitude, and emotional intelligence to lead others to success.
- Understand the interpersonal dynamics that will influence how well the leader or management team will work together and with the investors.
- Maximize the strengths and mitigate the risks of key players through laser-focused interventional training and development or coaching.

What would happen if an investor's portfolio could produce a few more home runs (10x ROI) and make a lot more base hits (3x to 8x ROI)? Do the math and you'll discover that a slight improvement in picking even moderate winners can substantially increase and even double the aggregate IRR of the portfolio.

This is what VQ profiling and applying axiogenic principles can do. It completely changes the paradigm; it loads the "dice" for the investor. In the words of one investor, "I'd rather have an 'A' team with a 'C' product than a 'C' team with an 'A' product."

Assessing VQ allows us to:

- Validate that 'A' teams really are 'A' teams
- Identify teams that *appear* to be 'B' or 'C' teams (based on history), but may actually be 'A' teams (based on VQ)
- Identify which B, and even C teams, could be turned into 'A' Teams through coaching and development

Through VQ profiling, we may even be able to rescue portfolio companies that are currently underperforming and at risk of failure. In a matter of a few hours, the underlying root cause of the underperformance can be identified. Then, the problem can be addressed by applying axiogenic principles (assuming the business product or service is viable). This sometimes requires the willingness of the major players, including the investors themselves, to engage in the turnaround process.

The goal is to increase the investor's ability to make sure they're putting their money and expertise into the best possible opportunities. In addition to the obvious financial advantages, it also mitigates risk, maximizes capital efficiency, optimizes the utilization of resources, and generates the greatest possible net value for everyone: investors, entrepreneurs, employees, the community, and the society as a whole.

For many early-stage investors, the motivation for a good ROI is not always about personal financial gain. Instead, it's about giving back. Such investors want to help entrepreneurs be successful, and getting a sufficient return on investment allows even more entrepreneurs to get the help they need. Talk about continuous value creation!

A valuegenic approach helps to maximize the yield produced with the "seed" money, experience, skills, connections and other resources that investors plant in the fields of entrepreneurial dreams. The value of this approach lies not just in the financial rewards, but also in the abundance that is created when more entrepreneurs are able to build successful businesses. When new ideas, inventions, and services are made manifest and available, these successful enterprises will employ and empower more people and add greater value to their customers.

Conclusion

If you are part of an investment group or a fund that needs to attract other investors, Axiogenics can give you a competitive edge. Your due diligence will be superior, your success rate will be higher, and you will exude more confidence to both investees and other potential investors. You will develop a reputation for doing things right and more

people will want to be a part of that—including more entrepreneurs—
and your deal-flow will increase as well.

• • •

The Valuegenic Entrepreneur

> To the valuegenic entrepreneur, The Central Question not only
> drives them personally, it drives their entire business.

> "Entrepreneurial profit is the expression of the value of what the
> entrepreneur contributes to production."
>
> *Joseph A. Schumpeter*

An entrepreneur is "a person who organizes and manages any enterprise,
especially a business, usually with considerable initiative and risk."[46]
We find that there are essentially two types of entrepreneurs: the
self-centric and the valuegenic. Either type can be successful in business; however, in our research the valuegenic entrepreneur succeeds
much more often and at a higher level *everywhere in their life*.

Let's look at some of the challenges that low-VQ perspectives can
create for entrepreneurs, including what might drive them to start their
own business to begin with.

Unfortunately, the "idea" of being an entrepreneur and the "reality"
of being an entrepreneur are often very different. A desire to find a
"short cut" to achieving their vision of success attracts many people to
entrepreneurship. Others want to escape the "oppressive authority" of a
boss looking over their shoulder, or the daily grind of memos, quotas,
meetings, deadlines, and paperwork. Some simply want to stop doing
the things they don't want to do; they just want to do things that are fun
and exciting. Of course, the idea of making more money and working
fewer hours is also attractive.

---

[46] Entrepreneur. Dictionary.com. *Dictionary.com Unabridged.* Random House, Inc.
http://dictionary.reference.com/browse/Entrepreneur
(accessed: April 19, 2010).

However, our assessment experience reveals that over 80% of these people have at least one of the following low-VQ challenges:

- **Unrealistic expectations with insufficient understanding of the process for achieving success.** While dreams and expectations can be highly motivating, if a business owner is overly focused on the fantasy of what success will give them, rather than on the process of creating success through the creation of value, failure is the more likely outcome.

  A valuegenic entrepreneur focuses on the process of value generation rather than the outcomes of fantasy.

- **Perfection at the cost of effectiveness.** Perfectionism can trap people in an endless effort to develop a "perfect" product or service, business plan, marketing brochure, or sales presentation. Sometimes, they never get around to actually doing the business of producing, marketing, selling and presenting a "good" product or service.

  A valuegenic entrepreneur focuses on balancing and optimizing their time, energy and resources to take the actions, produce the results, and acquire all the attributes of a successful businessperson.

- **Undervaluing one's own strengths, abilities or talents, and/or feeling a need to seek approval, rewards or recognition from outside oneself.** Low VQs in the self-view domain can cause one to focus more on what others think about them than on how they can best serve. This can create a need to impress others, to look good, or to be seen as being better than they believe themselves to be. At the same time, stopped by self-doubt, fear of failure, and their perceived "weaknesses," they are unable or unwilling to take actions that could genuinely be impressive.

A valuegenic entrepreneur is focused on using and developing their strengths to create value. They know that rewards and recognition are the natural outcome of the Process of Continuous Value Generation.

- **Connecting one's beliefs, ideas and opinions with one's own self worth.** Success can easily be undermined when a self-righteous and/or self-protective need to be right gets in the way of people, productivity and profit.

A valuegenic entrepreneur has little or no need to be right, only to generate value.

- **A desire for instant gratification and a disdain for doing things that require persistence and determination.** This mindset, if allowed to dominate choices, will sabotage success almost every time. Every business requires that things get done that the entrepreneur may not see as fun and exciting, and very few businesses become "over-night" successes.

A valuegenic entrepreneur engages in creating processes and systems that ensure that whatever needs to be done to maximize value (success) and minimize risk (failure) is done, even if they have to do it themselves.

Based on our experience, for example, almost everyone who enrolls in network marketing (MLM) opportunities have at least two of the above challenges. Is it any wonder that only a tiny fraction of network marketing "entrepreneurs" ever earn enough to make a living? This huge failure rate is not because these people are not capable of success or even that the business of network marketing isn't viable. The problem is that people with these low-VQ challenges are at risk of being overly enthralled by the possibility of wealth and freedom and don't fully understand the realities of what it takes to be successful. Unfortunately, unscrupulous "leaders" in the network marketing industry all too often exploit people with these challenges as a means of attracting them into their business.

Of course, network marketing is only one form of entrepreneurialism. Many who accept the challenge of being an entrepreneur value self-determination and take on both their daily work and their destiny with passion and purpose. They recognize that entrepreneurial success can be just as difficult and stressful, if not more, than a typical 9-5 job. Even so, any of these low-VQ challenges can sabotage their success for all the reasons we've discussed.

When people are locked into one or more of these low-VQ thought processes, they are generally unaware of it. They may stay stuck in the control of these low VQs until the negative results they're getting force them to examine why they have been unable to create greater success in their business and/or personal lives.

One of the greatest challenges for entrepreneurs, at least initially, is that they need to play every position on "the team" and accept sole responsibility for creating, building, maintaining and growing their enterprise. Playing every position demands a wide variety of strengths, often requiring them to perform tasks that may not come naturally. Very few people have the natural talent to play every position well. This can become an even bigger challenge as their enterprise grows. Growth creates the need for change and for developing different skills and greater decision-making capacities.

The good news is that, more often than not, people have more natural talent and untapped strengths than they realize, or even know how to utilize effectively.

A valuegenic approach to entrepreneurism changes everything. Consider the four core principles of Axiogenics:

1. Value drives success in all endeavors
2. Your mind-brain is already value-driven
3. There is a universal Hierarchy of Value
4. Accurately answering The Central Question is the key to maximizing your success.

To the valuegenic entrepreneur, The Central Question not only drives them personally, it drives their entire business. They do not allow their low VQs to get in the way of their success. They have a realistic understanding of their strengths (high VQs) and use them to their maximum advantage.

Now consider the power that engaging in SMART practice could bring to an entrepreneur:

Set Your Intentions
Maximize Your Mindfulness
Activate Your Strengths
Reconcile Gaps
Take Action

Is there any doubt that these are important keys to entrepreneurial success? Whether building a small or large enterprise, doing it from a valuegenic perspective keeps them focused on how they can create the greatest value. While the "size" of their endeavor will dictate the scope and complexity of the challenges they will face, the "size" of their VQ will determine their capacity to meet those challenges effectively.

The vision of the valuegenic entrepreneur goes beyond building a successful enterprise for their own benefit. They see themselves in partnership with their employees, stakeholders, customers, and community; ever striving to add greater value for all, leaving a legacy greater than themselves. To such an entrepreneur, axiogenic principles are not just slogans; they are the underlying motivation that fuels the fire of passion, purpose, and partnership.

"Too many of us are not living our dreams because we are living our fears."

~ Les Brown

. . .

The Valuegenic Relationship

Choose your partner wisely. If you already have a partner, wisely, choose the partner you have.

"A loving relationship is one in which the loved one is free to be himself—to laugh with me, but never at me; to cry with me, but never because of me; to love life, to love himself, to love being loved. Such a relationship is based upon freedom and can never grow in a jealous heart."

~ Leo F. Buscaglia

A valuegenic relationship is magical! First and foremost, it's a committed partnership for creating an extraordinary life together. The foundation of the extraordinary relationship is love and respect for the intrinsic value of each person above all else. Each partner brings a high level of awareness to the needs of the other and actively looks for opportunities to add value to the other. Each gives unconditionally to the other. Each holds the other accountable, in a bold, yet loving way for answering The Central Question and doing the work to raise their VQ.

In a valuegenic relationship, trust and faith in each other's intention to add value is ever-present, even if it seems to get lost from time to time in the hustle and bustle of life. Their communications always start in the intrinsic, then move to the extrinsic, and then finally deal with any systemic issues.

Valuegenic partners work diligently to recognize and reconcile any gap between them. They are constantly working to bring value *to* the relationship not just get value *from* the relationship. They live and breathe a very special Central Question:

> *"What choice can I make and action can I take,*
> *in this moment, to unleash the greatest net value*
> *in my partner's life and in our relationship?"*

• • •

The Valuegenic Parent

> Your family of origin does not need to be the model for the family YOU originate.

Valuegenic parents live, breathe, and model an omnipresent desire to answer The Central Question in every aspect of family life. They teach by example and, in so doing, they unleash the highest potential in both themselves and their children.

Such parents teach these principles to their children just as diligently as they might teach moral or religious Values, counting, the alphabet, handling finances, or driving a car.

Valuegenic parents encourage their children to ask The Central Question and to look at things from multiple perspectives. They work to help their children develop the capacity and wisdom to make good choices in their lives.

> One of my children was making life decisions that, as far as I could see, were only leading to trouble. My heart was fearful and I blamed myself for being a poor parent. The harder I tried to impose my will and push her in the "right" direction, the harder she pushed back and rebelled. Thanks to a conversation with my brother, which helped me to look at the situation from a different perspective, I was able to step back and apply some of the very principles you are reading about here.

I saw that I was more concerned about my own self-image, getting my way, and succeeding as a "good" parent (I didn't want to be embarrassed by having a wayward child) than I was about really understanding what she was going through, or how she perceived her world. My low VQs were causing me to be self-centric even though, to an observer, I might have been doing what any parent would do. My "intentions" were good, but it wasn't working.

My daughter could sense that I wasn't really interested in hearing her perspective. To her I was just being authoritative. She rebelled—sometimes outwardly, but more often, covertly.

With this new insight and a renewed commitment to being an *effective* valuegenic parent, I consciously chose to make it safe for her to explore her own value structure by treating her with love and respect, rather than an attitude of superior wisdom.

Eventually, she discovered, for herself, that her own value perceptions were limiting her options and possibilities in life. She started to be more deliberate and valuegenic in her choices. I'll never forget the day she said, without prompting, "Dad, I'm beginning to think that you might be much wiser than I've allowed myself to accept. I think I should listen to you more often."

What parent wouldn't want to hear those words? The truth is, however, the shift she made on her own has resulted in, at least in my view, a significant improvement in the decisions she is making for herself. She calls often for advice, but really, it's to use me as a trusted confidant. She doesn't really *need* my "advice" nearly as much as I used to try to impose it on her.

"Each day of our lives we make deposits in the memory banks of our children."

~ Charles R. Swindoll

What daily deposits are you making in your children's bank of value? Valuegenic parents model axiogenic principles in every aspect of family life. Each action and interaction places a small deposit in the minds of their children. These deposits will grow and multiply in incalculable ways. The quality of their "bank account" will determine, to a great degree, the life they create for themselves. Will the deposits you make in your children's minds grow into a trust fund of abundant wisdom or will they fester into a black hole of self-doubt, self-centric concerns, and scarcity? The choice is yours!

• • •

The Valuegenic Politician

If we want valuegenic politicians in office, we must first become valuegenic in the voting booth.

Oh, what a world it would be if all our politicians were valuegenic! What would be possible if politicians looked at governance not as a way to attain power through the control of value, but as a way to create greater value through empowerment?

A valuegenic politician would run for office to serve, not to be served. They would not be overly concerned about re-election, power, influence, or financial gain; they would be concerned with answering The Central Question according to the Hierarchy of Value.

A valuegenic politician would look at a bill or a law and ask first, 'What is the purpose of this bill? Is the intention and purpose of this law congruent with the Hierarchy of Value?' Next, they would ask, 'Does this bill create a system or policy that allows us to make better use of resources and improve the overall net quality of life for ALL people?'

Of course, such an approach would not and should not eliminate the need for honest debate over differences of opinion. Honest debate is good. A valuegenic approach doesn't eliminate the need for gain-gain negotiation. Yet even the process of political negotiation and reconciliation of gaps in perspectives, perceptions, and ideology would become more about co-creating value than getting re-elected. Rather than the systemic, politically motivated, power-grabbing compromises we see today, perhaps we'll see a return to governance for the people, rather than for the politicians.

A valuegenic politician will never forget their solemn duty to serve the people they represent. Above all, such a politician knows that the ultimate purpose of government is not to limit freedoms, but to protect, defend, and empower the full potential of its people to improve the quality of their life.

In addition to The Central Question, the words below will never wander too far from the politician's conscious mind:

> "We hold these truths to be self-evident, that all men are created equal, that they are endowed by their Creator with certain unalienable Rights, that among these are Life, Liberty and the pursuit of Happiness."
>
> ~ from the American Declaration of Independence

Wouldn't you like to know the VQs of some of our politicians? Should we ask politicians to attend courses on how to govern valuegenically rather than self- or power-centrically?

The Founding Fathers of America clearly placed the intrinsic power of the people above the systemic powers of the State. Who will be the first politicians to step up to valuegenic leadership? Who will lay The Central Question, the Hierarchy of Value, and the Process of Continuous Value Generation upon the debate lectern as principles to guide us into the future?

> "What a man does for himself, dies with him. What he does for his community lives long after he's gone."
>
> ~ Theodore Roosevelt

. . .

CHAPTER
9

Final Thoughts

"One man is equivalent to all Creation.
One man is a World in miniature."

~ *Albert Pike*

"Never doubt that a small group of thoughtful, committed citizens can
change the world; indeed, it's the only thing that ever has."

~ *Margaret Mead*

From Challenge to Choice

> We will let the stories speak for themselves.

Life presents challenges. Some of them are rather mundane, like running out of milk. Some can be painful, life changing, and tragic, such as losing a job, the passing of a loved one, or a debilitating injury or illness. In such times, we may easily wallow in self-pity or view the world as hard and unfair: "Why me?" some would cry to the heavens.

> "Courage is not the absence of fear, but rather the judgment that something else is more important than fear."
>
> ~ Ambrose Redmoon

Below are four real-life examples. First, let's look at the challenges, and then we'll explore the choices they made for their lives.

The Challenges . . .

Margaret

When my (Peter's) first wife, Margaret, was diagnosed with breast cancer, she had a full mastectomy and precautionary chemotherapy. Every test showed they "got it all." She was a breast cancer survivor! Less than two years later, the cancer was back with a vengeance. Months later, it was clear that her journey on Earth would soon be over. What would the remainder of her life be about?

Myself (Peter)

The love of my life for 22 years was going to die. My dreams, my hopes, my future, my whole world was being ripped out of my heart and soul. This isn't the way it was supposed to be! We had grand plans for our "second life"—after the kids were off on their own. On top of my empathetic pain and sorrow for Margaret, I had my own pain to deal with, along with the anticipated burdens of being a single, middle-aged Dad. How would I ever move forward? How would I take care of my children, who Margaret had been homeschooling as a stay-at-home-mom? Would I ever know romantic, passionate love again?

Alice

Alice, a single mom in her early twenties, found herself faced with an ugly choice. She had been charged as a conspirator in a criminal case. One choice was to plead "no-contest" and accept a sentence of 5 years probation—no jail-time. With a felony record, however, she would lose her job and have a very difficult time finding another. How would she take care of her infant son? Her other choice was to fight the charges, go to court, and risk being found guilty, which could result in up to 5 years in jail away from her baby. Despite the prosecution's circumstantial evidence, she felt she could not risk going to jail and losing her son. She took the plea bargain. Now, with a criminal record, her career goals and aspirations are shattered. Her life has taken a major turn toward serious hardship. As a single mom, feeling helpless and hopeless, what can she do to meet this new challenge?

George

In his mid-fifties, George lost a leg in a car accident. He owned a small house-painting business and climbed up and down ladders all day. Without his leg, climbing ladders was too difficult and dangerous. He loved his work and painting was all he knew. He didn't have disability insurance and had three kids in or about to enter college. What would he do now?

The Choices . . .

Margaret never thought her cancer was a mistake. She knew and embraced the fact that it was part of her life journey. She had very high VQs where it mattered most. From the moment the terminal diagnosis was delivered, she made a commitment to creating value in her life, and in the lives of her loved ones, with whatever time she had left. She became an inspiration to hundreds of people. She did not become an advocate for breast cancer research, she become an advocate for love, acceptance, and facing life with grace. She *became* grace. She transcended self-centeredness and became valuegenic. I cannot tell you how much a gift this was to me and to everyone she touched. Grace became her legacy.

Through Margaret, I witnessed, more deeply than ever, the power of The Central Question and being valuegenic. Oh, I had my pain, my fears, and my loneliness: how would I possibly manage to raise my two young children, continue homeschooling them, run my company, and run the household? How could I have any hope of a life of my own? I was overwhelmed and scared. But the words she whispered often in her final days, "Pete, your best days are still ahead," were a constant reminder that it would be true only if I *chose* to make it true. It gave me faith, patience, and a sense of purpose that still carries me forward today. It took time and work, and it wasn't always easy or pretty.

One year later, Pam, the love of my "new" life, blessed me. We merged our households into a new home, our kids enrolled in a great public school, business was thriving, and my "best days" were clearly coming. I would have a "second life" after all.

Margaret faced death and I faced life as a widower. Alice faced life as a struggling, single mom with a felony record, no college, and poor job prospects, while George faced his disability and the loss of the only livelihood he ever knew. We'll tell you the rest of their stories in a moment. Little doubt you know someone who has faced similarly difficult challenges, perhaps even much worse. These are just four people's stories. Can you think of at least one such story to reflect on from your own life?

How is Axiogenics relevant in each of these cases? The first thing to understand is that axiology teaches us that every choice and action either adds or subtracts value. When challenging events occur, nothing we can do will change the event. All we can do is make a choice to either create value or take it away.

> "Every adversity, every failure, every heartache carries with it the
> seed of an equal or greater benefit."
>
> ~ Napoleon Hill

At first, Alice saw little hope. Her value-centeredness was low, and she was at the mercy of her lowest-VQ thinking. She could not see a pathway to a meaningful life. She doubted her worthiness as a mom. She was ashamed, angry with herself, and angry at the world. I worked to help her see that creating value is often just a matter of changing perspectives. It is not about "positive thinking," in any self-deceptive way (where 'positive' comes before thinking). It's really about using our ability to shift perspectives so you can see the paths and possibilities that are already there. It's about using your strengths to see how you can create value, rather than wallowing in your perceived failures and weaknesses.

We looked at her assessment and in a matter of minutes had her anchored in her high-VQ perspectives. I taught her The Central Question and the fundamentals of SMART practice. Almost instantly, she began to see ways she could make her life work better and how she might use her experiences in a productive way. She saw very clearly how her sabotaging thinking habits had wreaked havoc in her life and that she no longer had to be a victim of those old perceptions.

George's story, however, has a different ending. His story far predates my understanding of anything that's in this book. He was my employer on a summer job when I was in my early-twenties. George did not have the tools to see life any other way than how he had seen it for his entire adult life. He could not face his family or his friends without first deadening the wounds in his heart and ego with alcohol. He alienated everyone around him, lashing out in anger, self-pity, and shame. In his mind, if he could not make a living, he was worthless.

The last time I saw him, his family had left him and the bank was foreclosing on his house. He sat in his wheelchair, sweaty, dirty, unshaved, and disheveled with a half-empty bottle of cheap liquor in his hands. His answer to The Central Question was to wallow in self-pity and alcohol. When it came time for me to leave, with a slur in his raspy voice, he said, "Son, be careful—the world will f--- you every chance it gets." It was many years later that I remembered his words. They came roaring back to me, seemingly out of nowhere, in a moment of my own despair, when I was sure my world was about to come crashing down around me. Clear as a bell, I heard George speak those words in my head. Then, strangely, I remembered my response: "I'll do my best, George. But if it tries, maybe I can find a way to make love with it instead." With that, I picked myself up and never looked back. It's all a matter of perspective, is it not?

Ironically, as I sit here writing these very words, George's old house (where I last saw him 30 years ago) is only a few hundred yards away from me. Pam and I, quite coincidently, bought our home in the same neighborhood.

• • •

Welcome to the Age of Gen-V

A new age is upon us. Are you ready?

> "We cannot become what we want to be
> by remaining the way we are."
>
> ~ Max DePree

Our world is changing. People are no longer satisfied with the pursuit of material wealth; they want more—more meaning, more purpose, more connection, more spiritual fulfillment, more peace and serenity—more of the intrinsic rewards of life.

The recent global economic crisis has awakened people to the reality that material success is fleeting and gives a false sense of security. Basic human values are moving to the forefront of our collective dreams and aspirations. As the GPWI studies suggest, organizations must address these changing needs for both their employees and their customers if they are to thrive in the 21st century.

At the same time, technology has, as Thomas Friedman in *The World is Flat* (2005) states, flattened our world and connected us in the common brotherhood of humanity. The terrorists are losing their war and goodness is gaining ground.

According to Daniel Pink, in *A Whole New Mind* (2006), we are moving out of the information age and into "The Conceptual Age." He writes, "The dominance of left-brain thinking (logical, rational, sequential) is coming to an end as right-brained thinking (empathy, creativity, synthesis) becomes more and more important."

In his most recent book, *Drive: The Surprising Truth About What Motivates Us*, Daniel Pink presents a powerful body of scientific evidence that clearly supports what we've been discussing in this book. He says that "intrinsic motivation" is more powerful than "extrinsic motivation." Sound familiar?

The shift to a value-based approach to life is further evidenced by the popularity of books that give hope, purpose, and meaning to life: Daniel Goleman's *Emotional Intelligence* and *Social Intelligence*; Eckhart Tolle's *A New Earth* and *The Power of Now*; Pastor Rick Warren's *The Purpose Driven Life*; and Marcus Buckingham's *First Break All the Rules* and *Now, Discover Your Strengths*; *The Speed of Trust* by Stephen M.R. Covey; *The Four* (and *Five*) *Agreements* by Don Miguel Ruiz; to name just a few.

What does all this add up to? We believe we are entering the age of "Gen-V"—an age when generating greater value is the central theme of success in life, love and leadership.

Axiogenics could not come at a more crucial time in human history. We need leaders who understand the importance of answering The Central Question: who are committed to valuegenic personal (self) leadership as well as organizational leadership. We need leaders who will stand up to the prevailing win-lose paradigm of business and politics to embrace a valuegenic paradigm that naturally produces abundance through gain-gain solutions. We need leaders who recognize that our future depends upon our collective ability to engage in the process of continuous value generation for all people, not just for a few. We need leaders who will strive to create profits through an abundance of valuegenic commitment, rather than self-centric desires. We need leaders who can spearhead efforts to educate, mentor, train, and coach a new generation of leaders, employees, partners, and stakeholders in accordance with the natural Hierarchy of Value.

Within the hearts and minds of humankind is an immeasurable reserve of cooperation, creativity, ingenuity, generosity, passion, compassion, and productivity. We must not waste this extraordinary natural and precious resource.

We need only to liberate this potential by raising our standards, celebrating the human spirit, and setting aside our petty, self-centric agendas long enough to open ourselves up to the possibility of discovering new and better answers to The Central Question. No individual truly aspires to mediocrity, though fear and self-doubt may hold him back. What good employer, parent, or spouse would not want to see the unique and precious gifts of all people unleashed?

Our mission is to spread this message to as many current and future leaders as possible. Our vision is a world in which every human being lives and works in an environment that celebrates their uniqueness and encourages them to achieve their fullest potential.

If we succeed, history will look back to our generation as a turning point for humanity; an age when our ethics finally caught up with our technology and opened the floodgates of creativity to create an abundance greater than any other in human history. We could end widespread hunger and abject poverty. We could eliminate unhealthy conflict and still honor competition and individualism as a force for greater creativity, quality, and service. We could accelerate technology without fear of losing our moral and ethical foundations. Healthcare costs could go down and wellness could go up. We could reduce crime, abuse, and prejudice. We could fulfill the greatest dreams mankind has ever envisioned for the future of our world.

"What lies behind us and what lies before us are tiny matters compared to what lies within us."

~ Ralph Waldo Emerson

Axiogenics unleashes the extraordinary pent-up brilliance awaiting liberation within each of us. It aligns us with the universal flow. When we are valuegenic, we enter into an exquisite partnership with the world around and within us. In this partnership, the world becomes an extension of us and we become an extension of the world. We become a part of something bigger than ourselves: we become bigger than we ever knew we could be.

"The surest way to happiness is to lose yourself in a cause greater than yourself."

~ Unknown

Through Axiogenics, we have the science-based means to help ourselves and others align with the natural order of value, to transcend our limits of the past, and to create a brighter future.

We invite—in fact, we implore you—to make the deliberate choice to become more valuegenic; to step up to valuegenic leadership and to help others do the same.

If you get nothing else from this book, we hope that you will keep The Central Question in the forefront of your mind and make it the primary perspective from which you approach everything you think and do. Continually develop your ability to answer this question well, and by this practice alone, you will be living the heart and science of generating value.

**What choice can I make and action can I take,
in this moment, to create the greatest net value?**

Bibliography

Amazon.com, E. (n.d.). *A Q&A with Jonah Lehrer, Author of How We Decide.* Retrieved April 4, 2010, from Amazon.com: http://www.amazon.com/How-We-Decide-Jonah-Lehrer/dp/0618620117/ref=sr_1_1?ie=UTF8&qid=1270506789&sr=8-1

Amen, D. G. (2005). *Making a Good Brain Great.* New York: Random House.

Axiology, Journal of Formal, multiple editions, 2008-2010: Robert S. Hartman Institute, Rem B Edwards, Senior Editor

Beauregard Ph.D., M., & O'Leary, D. (2007). *The Spiritual Brain.* New York, NY: HarperOne.

Buckingham, M., & Coffman, C. (1999). *First Break All The Rules.* New Yourk: Simon & Schuster.

Buckinghamn, M., & Clifton, D. o. (2001). *Now, Discover Your Strengths.* New York: Simon & Schuster.

Colvin, G. (2008, October 21). Why Talent is Overrated. *Fortune* .

Conner, K. T. (2009). Innovation: An Axiological and OD Exploration. *Journal of Formal Axiology: Theory and Practice* , 41-54.

Covey, S. R. (2004). *The 7 Habits of Highly Effective People.* New York: Free Press.

Covey, S. R. (2004). *The Eighth Habit.* New York: Free Press.

David Mefford, P. (2009). Formal Axiology: Philosophy or Science? *Journal of Formal Axiology: Theory and Practice* , 2, 111-129.

David, V., & Vouimba, R.-M. (2009). Clues on the organizing effect of reward-predictive cues:... *Cell Science Review* , 5 (5), 21-29.

Demarest, Peter; Schoof, Harvey; Blanchard, David . (2008). *Neuro-Axiology: A Foundation for Value-Centered Leadership and Organizational Tranformation.* Bountiful, UT: 6 Advisors, Inc.

Doidge, N. (2007). *The Brain That Changes Itself.* New York: Penguin Books.

Ericsson, K. A., Krampe, R. T., & Tesch-Romer, C. (1993). The Role of Deliberate Practice in the Acquisition of Expert Performance. *Psychological Review , 100* (3), 363-406.

Frida E. Polli, C. I. (2009). Hemispheric Differences in Amygdala Contributions to Response Monitoring. *NeuroReport , 20,* 398-402.

Friedman, T. L. (2005). *The World is Flat.* New York: Farrar, Straus and Giroux.

Gladwell, M. (2005). *Blink: The Power fo Thiking Without Thinking.* New York, NY: Little, Brown and Company.

Goleman, D. (1995). *Emotional Intelligence.* New York: Bantam Books.

Goleman, D. (2006). *Social Intelligence.* New York: Random House.

Great Place to Work Institute - Financial Results. (n.d.). Retrieved September 25, 2009, from Great Place to Work Institute: http://www.greatplacetowork.com/great/graphs.php

Great Place to Work Institute - Results. (n.d.). Retrieved September 25, 2009, from Great Place to Work Institute: http://www.greatplacetowork.com/great/results.php

Greenleaf, R. K. (2002). *Servant Leadership.* New York: Paulist Press.

Gurau, M. (2006, November 6). *Entrepreneur, Coach Thyself.* Retrieved from http://www.clearvcs.com/_downloads/VBC_MHG_110606.pdf

Gurau, M. (2010, February 17). *Failure comes with the venture capitalist's job.* Retrieved April 16, 2010, from Mass High Tech, The Journal of New England Technology: http://www.masshightech.com/stories/2010/02/15/weekly3-Failure-comes-with-the-venture-capitalists-job.html

Hartman, R. S. (1991). Applications of the Science of Axiology. In R. B. Edwards, J. W. Edwards, R. B. Edwards, & J. W. Davis (Eds.), *Forms of Value and Valuation: Theory and Applications* (pp. 193-209). Lanham, MA: University Press of America.

Hartman, R. S. (1994). *Freedom to Live: The Robert Hartman Story.* (A. R. Ellis, Ed.) Amsterdam: Rodopi B.V.

Hartman, R. S. (1963, January 14). *The Individual in Management.* Retrieved October 27, 2009, from The Robert Hartman Institute: http://www.hartmaninstitute.org/html/IndividualInManagement.htm

Hartman, R. S. (1967). *The Stucture of Value.* Carbondale, Il: Southern Illinois University Press.

Hartman S. Hartman Institure. http://www.hartmaninstitute.org

Lama, H. H. (2005). *The Universe in a Single Atom.* New York: Broadway Books.

Lipton, B. H. (2009). *The Biology of Belief* (5th ed.). Calsbad, CA: Hay House, Inc.

Pert, C. B. (1997). *Molecules of Emotion.* New York: Scribner.

Pink, D. H. (2005). *A Whole New Mind.* New York: Penguin.

Pink, D. H. (2009). *Drive.* New York: Penguin.

Pomeroy, L. (2005). *Th New Science of Axiological Psychology.* Amsterdam-New York: Rodopi.

Pugh, G. E. (1977). *The Biolgical Origins of Human Values.* New York: Basic Books.

Schwartz, J., Stapp, H., & Beauregard, M. (2005, June). *Quantum physics in neuroscience and psychology.* Retrieved January 2010, from http://www-physics.lbl.gov/~stapp/PTRS.pdf

Schwartz, M. J., Begley, S., & Begley, S. (2002). *The Mind & The Brain.* New York: HarperCollins.

Sperry, R. (1974). Messages from the Laboratory. *Engineering and Science* (Special Issue on behavioral biology).

St. Jacques, P., Delcos, F., & Cabeza, R. (2010). Effects of aging on functional connectivity of the amygdala during negative evaluation: A network analysis of fMRI data. *Neurobiology of Aging , 31* (2), 315-327.

Strauch, B. (2010). *The Secret Life of the Grown-Up Brain.* Viking Press.

Tolle, E. (2005). *A New Earth.* New Yourk: Penguin.

Tolle, E. (1999). *The Power of Now.* Vancouver, BC: Namaste Publishing.

Warren, R. (2002). *The Purpose Drive Life.* Frand Rapid, MI: Zondervan.

Wikipedia. (2010, March 6). *Renaissance.* Retrieved March 6, 2010, from http://en.wikipedia.org/wiki/Renaissance

Williamson, M. (1992). A Return to Love: Reflections on the Principles of "A Course in Miracles". In *A Return to Love: Reflections on the Principles of "A Course in Miracles".* Harper Collins.

Woods, G., & Zito, K. (2009). Changes in synaptic morphology associated with LTD.. *Cell Science Reviews , 5* (3), 7-13.

Zimmer, C. (2009, May). The Brain. *Discover ,* pp. 28-29.

Zimmer, C. (2009, September). The Brain. *Discover ,* pp. 30-31.

Index

P

R

S

About Peter D. Demarest

 Since his early teens, selling skin-care products, Burpee Seeds, and lawn-care services door-to-door, Peter has been a street-student of the successful mind. His path has taken many twists and turns across the peaks and valleys of life. After serving in the U.S. Navy Submarine Service, most of his "first-life" career was spent in the information technology industry. He held a variety of positions from geek to guru in the both the corporate and the entrepreneurial worlds.

In the early 2000s, around the time his wife was diagnosed with breast cancer, he left the corporate world to pursue his passion for transformational coaching and education. Always driven by a thirst for what he calls *practical enlightenment* (the elimination of the time between when you screw up and when you realize it), he dove deeply into the fields of neuroscience and axiology.

Over the years, he has trained dozens of other coaches in axiology-based coaching and has personal coached, trained and consulted with hundreds of people including doctors, lawyers, entrepreneurs, CPAs, managers and executives of numerous organizations small and large.

Today, as a thought-leader in the integration of axiology and neuro-science and creator of the concept of Axiogenics, he and his partners in *Axiogenics, LLC* are on a mission to bring this work to other visionary leaders through speaking, consulting, training, coaching and writing.

His first wife, Margaret passed away of breast cancer in 2004. Blessedly he is now remarried to the love of his "second-life," Pam, with a blended family of five children, one grandchild, and a number of dogs, cats, chickens and fish. They live in Pennsylvania.

About Harvey J. Schoof

Since age 19, when he taught his first class of fifty third-graders, Harvey has been involved in the work of educating, counseling, training and coaching. He has worked as a rehabilitation counselor, manager, and HR professional as well as an instructor of management and organizational communication at seven different colleges and universities.

He is a founding member of the *daVinci Charter School Academy*, where he served as the board president for 12 years, as well as a founding board member of the *Michigan Association of Charter School Boards*.

Over the past 30 years, Harvey has become an acclaimed expert in the science of Axiology, training coaches and other practitioners from across the United States, Canada, the UK and the Netherlands.

Throughout his consulting and coaching career, Harvey has worked with hundreds of companies and thousands of managers, sharing his insights and experiences to assist them in becoming more valuegenic in their personal and professional lives.

Harvey has joined with Peter Demarest and Traci Duez, as a founding partner of *Axiogenics, LLC*.

He lives in Michigan with his wife Jan. They have three wonderful children and six awesome grandchildren.

Acknowledgements

From Peter Demarest...

Words cannot adequately express my gratitude to you, Harvey, for being the greatest collaborator, co-creator, and business partner anyone could hope for.

Thanks also to Traci Duez, Lincoln Holbrook, Vernon Castleton, Lynne Klippel, Dr. Pat Gayman, Susan Kaminga, my father Don, my brother Jim, and my daughter Hannah for their invaluable input and feedback.

To my late wife, Margaret, I offer my eternal gratitude. Among her final words she said to me, "Pete, your best days are still ahead." With these words, she inspired me with her conviction that my journey, my life's mission, would not and could not die with her; that to honor her legacy, I must also honor all the potential that God has given me, diligently live these extraordinary principles, and give myself fully to my "second life." Her words have rung true and this book is my testimony.

To my sister, Sue Ridgway, you may never know how often those few simple words you spoke to me many years ago have echoed in my ears. In some of my darkest hours, they have given me solace, confidence, and inspiration.

Above all, I thank Pam, my extraordinary wife and "second-life" partner who rescued me from the fate of a lonely widower. Who, with the patience of an Angel, the faith of a saint, and the encouragement of an Olympic coach, enabled and inspired me to do this work. Thank you, love, for your all your support, hard work, and wise counsel.

From Harvey Schoof...

I want to take this opportunity to thank my loving wife Jan for making the last 45 years a wonderful and joyful experience. Without her willingness to take me on as a life-long project, always supporting, encouraging and guiding me to grow and explore new possibilities, I would most certainly not be where I am today.

I also what to thank a number of people who have, at major turning points in my life, been there to mentor, teach, listen and even push me to take on new challenges. So, my heartfelt "thank you" to my late and dear friend Walt Reynolds for opening my eyes to a world of awe, to Wayne Carpenter for sharing his wisdom, to Chuck Jones for giving me the room to pursue my dreams, to Matt Farner for his generosity in helping me explore possibilities, to Doug Langham for being an example of valuegenic living, and to Dave Molinaro for always being my friend.

My thanks, also, to all of you who have believed in me and given me the privilege to have been your teacher, coach and friend.

The Central Question of
Life, Love and Leadership:

**What choice can I make and action can I take,
in this moment, to create the greatest net value?**

Learn to answer this question
and your life will be transformed!

What's Your VQ?

Made in the USA
Lexington, KY
14 September 2014